Beatrice Trum Hunter's Favorite Natural Foods

ADAPTED FROM A SERIES OF PROGRAMS

ON WGBH, BOSTON

Simon and Schuster   New York

Designed by Irving Perkins
Manufactured in the United States of America
By The Book Press, Inc.

1   2   3   4   5   6   7   8   9   10

Library of Congress Cataloging in Publication Data

Hunter, Beatrice Trum.
    Beatrice Trum Hunter's Favorite Natural Foods.

    "Adapted from a series of programs on WGBH, Boston."
    1. Cookery.   2. Marketing (Home economics)
I.   Title.
TX715.H898   641.5   74–10749
ISBN 0–671–21820–4

To the dedicated television staff at WGBH, Boston, whose enthusiastic support made it possible to launch this series of programs successfully

Contents

✤

Foreword

✲

Before my series on WGBH in Boston, I had made many television appearances in interviews and panel discussions, but the preparation of natural foods in front of a television camera proved to be an entirely new experience. It seemed formidable— I would be in front of the camera, solo. It would be my responsibility to write and edit the scripts, help buy the needed equipment and food ingredients. On the show, I would demonstrate cooking techniques clearly while matching the dialogue to what I did, all the while smiling at the camera while preparing foods and taking cues from time cards in order to end with split-second precision. It couldn't be done! How could I possibly demonstrate yogurt, sauerkraut, sprouts, sourdough and other homemade goodies in that incredibly short time slot? How could I ever sprout many kinds of seeds, each with their own germination schedule, and have them all ready, at their peak of perfection on the day of taping, or be certain that the sauerkraut would have stopped fermenting at the precise day when it would be needed? Uncontrollable! How could I ever learn within so short a time all of the special television techniques, so different from those I was used to with live audiences?

During rehearsals, there were a number of crises. The milk boiled over. An orange rolled off the table. A rubberband snapped unexpectedly. A shelf collapsed and shattered many pieces of crystal. I cut my finger, I tripped wires, I experienced an electrical shock. Every time we encountered such mishaps, we shuddered to think of their happening during the actual tapings.

From the programs' inception, the entire WGBH television staff showed enthusiasm for the project and sympathy for the developing starlet. They were tolerant of my many blunders and helpful in suggesting improvements. And everyone seemed to enjoy eating the samples of natural foods, prepared during numerous rehearsals.

At last, the tapings were to be made. Unforeseen crises arose, tragic at the time, but comic in retrospect. When the first taping went smoothly, I heaved a deep sigh of relief, letting out pent-up anxiety. Then, I was asked if I would be willing to retape the program. Although my own performance had gone smoothly, the color had not mixed well, and at times I appeared quite green on the tape. We referred to that taping as "The Green Giantess."

When we were ready to tape the program on Confections, I discovered that the almonds which I had blanched at five A.M. for pressing into the unbaked fruitcake had mysteriously disappeared from the table. A staff member admitted thinking those almonds were leftovers; he had snacked on them. The entire production was held up while he hand-whittled the skins off of more almonds.

During the opening sequence of the Sourdough program, I planned to hold an exceedingly long loaf of sourdough French bread. At the end of the sequence, I would slice some of it, butter it and eat it. We had to tape that program three times and by the third taping, the loaf was so sadly reduced in size, that I feared if we had to retape again, we would lose our opening prop!

I learned what is meant by "heightened reality" on television. In a last-minute panic, we were unable to find black bean soup or black beans in Boston, so I made a mixture of *miso* and water that *looked* like black bean soup. We also ran short of carob powder, so I substituted bitter chocolate. The staff had to be warned that the black bean soup and the confections were not highly edible. How we struggled to keep salad greens crisp under hot television lights, cooked broccoli steaming and bright green and frozen dessert the proper texture!

The outcome of these efforts was a series of sixteen programs demonstrating natural food preparation. To our knowledge this is the first television program of its kind which has ever been produced anywhere.

The response to these programs is heartwarming. It has been especially gratifying to read some of the fan mail: "I haven't decided how Beatrice Trum Hunter can pack so much information into such a short period of time. She's a marvel." "For years I have been interested in natural foods, but you've taught me many new things." "My husband never misses your programs, and he is very fussy. He always said, 'Never trust a woman with three names,' but you have made him change his mind." "Each program is a little gem." "The entire capsulated program, scrubbed of any superfluities, sparkles and shines!" "WGBH should be congratulated for putting on this program. I am revolted by the too often deadly gourmet concoctions on most cooking shows. Beatrice Trum Hunter shows clearly and briefly what can be done with nutritious ingredients. Her few minutes deserve the Pulitzer prize, or whatever it is TV gets."

One note, especially, caught my attention. "The Beatrice Trum Hunter's Natural Foods show is great—a good beginning. How about more philosophy, more reasons why, and of course, more time!" In response to this request I wrote this book, which is an adaptation of the television programs, and an attempt to give more philosophy, more reasons why, and of course, more time to the subject. May it satisfy all those television viewers who wanted more information, as well as a larger, growing audience of individuals who would like to learn more about natural foods.

—BEATRICE TRUM HUNTER

1 Vegetables, Vegetables

✿

Nutritionists tell us that it is wise to eat a wide variety of foods day by day. By doing so, we have a good opportunity to get all of the nutrients our bodies need to maintain health. In all parts of the United States we are blessed with a great assortment of vegetables from which to choose throughout the year.

If you encounter unfamiliar vegetables while shopping, develop a spirit of adventure. Be willing to buy and try new ones. If you grow vegetables, try planting some that may be unfamiliar to you. These are a few of the less frequently used vegetables. How many have you tried?

Artichoke, French or globe: Look for compact, heavy globular buds with tightly closed leaf scale. If you find surface brown spots on the artichokes during the winter months it means the buds were touched by frost but the flavor will be unharmed. The artichoke's quality is unaffected by its size. You may have wanted to try artichokes but did not know how to prepare them. To start, just before you cook them, cut an inch off straight across the top of the buds and pull off the loose leaves around the bottom near the stem. Then clip off the spine tips with a pair of kitchen scissors. Slip the artichokes into boiling water and cover. Cook about twenty-five minutes, turning each one several times. Pierce the stem base with a fork to be sure the artichokes are tender. If not, cook longer. Drain them upside down. You can remove the "chokes," the threadlike parts in the center, with a spoon before serving or leave the chokes until later. A grapefruit spoon with a serrated edge is especially good. Serve hot or cold. Each person pulls off the petals one by one and draws them between the front teeth to scrape off and eat only the tender base part of the leaf. Discard the remainder of the leaf. Continue until you come to the fuzzy center or "choke." Discard it. Cut the base of the artichoke into bite-size pieces for easy eating. This base is the portion that is frequently marinated and known as "artichoke heart."

Artichoke, Jerusalem: This tuber has odd shapes. It looks like ginger root both in appearance and color. Select Jerusalem artichokes that are firm and free of mold. To prepare, scrub with a brush but do not peel them. Wash them thoroughly. When cooked, the flesh of Jerusalem artichokes tends to turn oyster gray in color. You can cut raw Jerusalem artichokes into slices or strips and add them to a tossed salad.

Cardoon or *Cardoni:* This vegetable looks like large stalks of celery with a gray-green bloom on the leaves and heart. Choose stalks that are free of blemishes and that have a fresh-looking bloom. Cardoon reaches the markets in fall and winter. When you are ready to use it, wash the stalks and cut off the prickly edges. Remove the strings from the stalks, since these cellulose strings do *not* soften during cooking.

Celeriac or *Celery root:* This root vegetable appears on the market from October through April. Select firm, clean celeriac. Wash and scrub it with a brush to remove all traces of dirt, leaves and rootlets. Leave unpeeled, cook until tender and then peel and slice it.

Fennel or *Finocchio* or *Anise:* This pearly-white bulb has bright-green featherlike leaves and a mild licorice flavor. It is sold from October to March. You can use fennel as a cooked vegetable, or as a raw one in tossed salad. Wash and scrape any blemishes from the bulb and prepare it as you would prepare celery. Fennel is considered to be a good source of vitamins A and C, with minor amounts of other nutrients.

Greens: Doubtless you use spinach. But have you tried other greens? If you purchase beets or turnips and are fortunate in having the crisp greens still intact on these root vegetables, by all means prevent the clerk at the check-out counter from cutting them off. Use them as a cooked vegetable. Chicory, collards, dandelion, kale, mustard and Swiss chard are other greens that reach markets at various times during the year. The best are those that look fresh, having tender green leaves with a bright color, and having a minimum of yellowed or wilted leaves. To prepare, cut off the roots and remove any damaged or yellowed leaves. Search for slugs or insects. Strip off the thick, stiff midribs, and wash the leaves thoroughly in cool running water. Save some of the very young tender raw leaves for tossed salad. Greens are considered to be a good source of vitamins A and C and a fair source of iron; and they have minor amounts of other vitamins and minerals. For individuals on low-sodium diets, turnip greens, low in sodium, are especially welcome.

Kohlrabi: These bulb vegetables appear on markets in summer and fall but they are at their peak of goodness in June and July. Look for small- to medium-size bulbs with fresh green leaves. When the bulbs grow very large their texture becomes woody. Avoid deeply scarred or blemished bulbs. To prepare kohlrabi, pare off the skin and wash the bulbs. Save the leaves if they are fresh and tender and cook them along with the bulbs. Young raw kohlrabi, peeled and sliced, is good in tossed salad.

Leek: Select bunches of bright green-topped leeks with white bulb bases. Cut off the tops and wash the bases. Make certain to remove all the dirt from crevices. Steam lightly as a vegetable, or use in soup.

Okra: Okra pods may appear on the market throughout the year, but the peak months are from June through November. Select crisp, bright-green pods, free of blemishes. The best okra pods are those that are small to medium in size. Wash and trim the stem end. Leave small pods whole, but cut large ones into half-inch slices. Cook as green beans and serve plain. Okra is an excellent thickener for homemade soups.

Rappini or *Rapini* or *Broccoli rabe* or *Raab:* This vegetable, with its fresh Kelly-green appearance and few buds, appears on markets in fall and winter. Remove any discolored stems and trim the roots. Parboil, drain and then prepare by braising, boiling or steaming. Rappini is considered to be a good source of vitamins A and C, with minor amounts of other vitamins and minerals.

Fresh vegetables are usually at their best quality and price at the peak of their season, when their supply is plentiful. But don't buy them simply because the price is low. Don't buy more vegetables than you can use without waste. Most fresh vegetables can be stored for two to five days, except for root vegetables, which can be stored from one to several weeks. (Guidelines for storage begin on p. 22.) It is penny wise but pound foolish to buy any vegetables already affected by decay. Spending a few extra cents for vegetables in prime condition may be a better bargain.

The United States Department of Agriculture (USDA) has defined differences in quality found in most fresh and processed vegetables with grade standards. Also, USDA administers a Federal-State Inspection Service to inspect and certify the quality of fresh vegetables according to its grade standards, and it maintains a staff of federal inspectors for processed vegetables.

However, the use of U.S. grade standards and inspection services by the vegetable industry is *voluntary*. Users must pay a fee for the inspection service. Although such grade standards and inspection services are used extensively by packers, processors, buyers and others involved in wholesale rating, shoppers in retail stores rarely find an indication of U.S. grades on fresh vegetables. A few states do require that certain products be graded and labeled, either on the basis of Federal or state grade standards.

You may find grade designations on packages of potatoes, onions, carrots and, occasionally, on packages of other fresh vegetables sold in retail stores. Unless these packages also bear the official USDA grade shield, or "Packed Under Continuous Inspection of the U.S. Department of Agriculture" or "USDA Inspected" the products have not been officially graded nor inspected.

The USDA grades for fresh vegetables are:

U.S. Fancy: This is the premium grade for some vegetables. Such vegetables have outstanding quality and appearance compared to what is usually available. Only a very small percentage of a crop meets the standards of this grade.

U.S. No. 1: This is the highest grade for most vegetables. In a normal year, about two thirds of a crop is labeled U.S. No. 1 grade. These vegetables are of high quality, they have a good appearance, and few defects.

U.S. No. 2 or *U.S. Combination:* These lower grades of fresh vegetables are not likely to appear in retail stores.

When you buy fresh vegetables, it is helpful to know the approximate amounts you will need. The following is an easy guide, giving you the amounts needed for six average servings of about ½-cup per person.

Artichoke, French or globe: 6 buds
Artichoke, Jerusalem: 1½ pounds
Asparagus: 2½ pounds for spears; 1¾ to 2 pounds for cuts and
　tips
Beans, lima: 2¾ pounds, in pods
Beans, snap: 2 pounds
Beets: 2½ pounds, or 3 bunches
Broccoli: 1¾ to 2 pounds
Brussels sprouts: 1¼ to 1½ pounds
Cabbage (green or red): 1¼ to 1½ pounds, shredded; 1½ to 2
　pounds, in wedges
Cardoon: 1 large stalk
Carrots: 1½ pounds
Cauliflower: 2 pounds, or 2 medium-size heads
Celeriac: 2 pounds
Celery: 1½ pounds or 1 large stalk
Corn: 6 to 12 ears
Eggplant: 2 pounds
Fennel: 6 medium-size bulbs
Greens: 2 to 3 pounds, untrimmed
Kohlrabi: 6 medium-size bulbs
Leeks: 3 bunches
Okra: 1¼ to 1½ pounds
Onions: 1¾ pounds
Parsnips: 1½ to 2 pounds
Peas: 3 pounds, in pods
Potatoes, sweet: 1½ pounds
Potatoes, white: 1½ pounds
Rappini: 2 pounds
Squash, summer, 1½ to 2 pounds
Squash, winter: 3 to 4 pounds
Tomatoes: 1¼ to 2 pounds
Turnips: 1¾ to 2 pounds

Shopping for Frozen Vegetables

You may think that fresh vegetables are more nutritious than processed ones. Correct? This assumption is widespread. While under ideal conditions it is true, under present conditions, this guideline is only generally accurate.

Fresh, locally grown, picked-when-ripe-and-rushed-to-market vegetables are best. But what happens when less than ideal conditions prevail? Fresh produce may be harvested in the west and shipped by train or truck several thousands of miles east. The days spent in transit inevitably cause some nutrient losses. Produce selected to survive this long journey may have been picked when immature and can reach its destination in an imperfect state of ripeness.

The freezing of vegetables offers a means of processing foods with minimal destruction, and at their peak of ripeness. Sweet corn and green peas are two notable examples of vegetables that retain their garden-fresh qualities better when they are frozen than when they are shipped long distances.

Some vegetables are available frozen but rarely found fresh at markets anymore. Lima beans are an example.

Some vegetables, such as okra, grown in the South and a staple of Southern cooking, may be found in the North now and then in frozen form, but rarely as a fresh vegetable.

If you live in a section of the country with cold winters, the supply of fresh produce reaching your market during the winter months may be quite limited. Frozen vegetables can supplement the supply of fresh ones at such times and add greater variety to your daily diet.

Like fresh vegetables, most frozen ones are packed and priced according to their quality, even if a grademark is not on the label. When vegetables are packed under continuous USDA inspection the individual package may carry the U.S. grademark. The USDA grades for frozen vegetables are:

U.S. Grade A or *U.S. Fancy:* These vegetables are carefully selected for color, tenderness and freedom from blemishes. They are the most tender, succulent and flavorsome ones produced, and are intended for meals where high quality is desired.

U.S. Grade B or *U.S. Extra Standard Grade B:* These vegetables may be of good quality but they are not selected as strictly for color and tenderness as U.S. Grade A. These are usually a little less tasty than U.S. Grade A, but suitable for casserole dishes.

U.S. Grade C or *U.S. Standard Grade C:* These vegetables are not so uniform in color, tenderness or flavor as those in higher grades. They are usually more mature, and considered a thrifty buy when appearance is not a prime factor, as in the case of soups, purées or soufflés. However, these vegetables cannot be considered as nutritionally prime.

The "Packed Under Continuous Inspection of the U.S. Department of Agriculture" shield may be shown along with the grade shield, or it may be shown by itself. Sometimes the grade name is indicated *without* the "U.S." before it, as "Fancy" or "Grade A." Any frozen vegetable bearing such a designation has *not* been *officially* inspected for grade but it *should* measure up to the stated quality.

If you are concerned about nutritional quality, as you should be, choose the best grades obtainable. Since many frozen vegetables sold in the retail stores will not bear grade designations, you should be guided by another factor. Many chain stores carry two or more quality products under their own private labels. The difference in price may indicate quality differences.

If you are budget-minded—and who is not these days?—be guided by the following:

Buy vegetables without added sauces or special flavorings. These elaborations add to the price, and anyway, the additions may contain undesirable ingredients. Whole frozen vegetables generally cost more than cut styles because it is hard to keep fragile vegetables whole during processing. Whole vegetables, uniform in size, may be attractive if they are used as a hot vegetable. This is true of beets, for example. But remember that such sizing adds to the cost of the processed product. Any vegetables that are fancy-cut, such as those sliced lengthwise (French-style green beans or julienne carrots) usually cost more than other cut styles. Short-cut green beans or diced carrots are the least expensive styles, and they do not compromise nutritional quality. These are suitable for stews, soups or soufflés. Keep this special nutritional note in mind when you select frozen asparagus: there is more ascorbic acid in the tips than in the butt ends.

In buying frozen vegetables, it is helpful for you to know the approximate amounts you need. Frozen vegetables have already been trimmed, so their volume will be less than fresh, unprocessed vegetables. In the case of leafy ones, such as frozen spinach, they will be considerably less bulky than their fresh counterparts. The following guide gives you the approximate amounts needed for six average servings of about ½ cup per person:

Asparagus, whole:	24 ounces, frozen		
Beans, lima:	16	"	"
Beans, snap, cut:	16	"	"
Broccoli, spears:	20	"	"
Brussels sprouts:	16	"	"
Carrots, sliced or diced:	16	"	"
Cauliflower:	20	"	"

Corn, whole kernel:	20 ounces, frozen	
Corn, on cob:	32	" "
Kale:	24	" "
Peas:	20	" "
Potatoes, small, whole:	21	" "
Spinach:	24	" "
Squash, summer, sliced:	24	" "
Turnip greens:	28	" "

Storing Fresh Vegetables

After you have carefully shopped for vegetables, treat them with loving care when you arrive home. Store them promptly and properly.

Remember that once vegetables have been picked, they begin to lose their value in two different ways. The first loss is the obvious physical one, when the edible parts, like the outer leaves of lettuce, are removed. The second loss is the more subtle chemical one that develops with changes in the plant tissue structure. Because respiration and enzyme activity continue in plants, the texture and vitamin content of some vegetables deteriorate rapidly. This is especially true if you store vegetables improperly, and at inappropriate temperatures. You will notice this loss when vegetables look wilted or limp, or when they become dry, brown or pale.

Also note that some vegetables are best stored with some humidity, while others do best in dry air. Some can be stored for only short periods, while others are more durable. Some do best stored in sun or in light, while others should be shielded from light. By learning the ideal storage conditions of different vegetables you can minimize their nutritional losses. Such information is important, and especially so in times of food shortages and high food prices.

By way of illustration, examine the subject of vitamin C, or ascorbic acid. In many reports on the changes of the nutrient composition in foods, ascorbic acid is the vitamin most frequently studied. Ascorbic acid is lost easily. It is both heat-sensitive and water-soluble. So, whatever measures you take to retain ascorbic acid in vegetables will usually help to protect the other nutrients as well.

Most of us depend largely on fresh vegetables (and fruits) for our daily supply of ascorbic acid. Produce contributes about 90 percent of all the ascorbic acid in the average American diet. Ascorbic acid is not manufactured in the human body, so we must obtain it from outside sources. For this reason, it is extremely important to conserve as much as possible of this nutrient in vegetables. How?

Refrigerate fresh vegetables such as salad greens, kale, spinach, turnip greens, chard and broccoli as soon as you bring them into the house. These vegetables will retain their nutrients best if you store them in high humidity, and at near freezing temperature. Use the vegetable crisper in the refrigerator.

Leafy, dark-green vegetables, as well as broccoli, will retain only about half of their total ascorbic acid after five days in your refrigerator if the temperature is between 40 and 50° F. Even after such a substantial loss of ascorbic acid, these vegetables are still considered to be excellent sources of ascorbic acid (and vitamin A) due to their high initial supply of it. Even after such loss, these vegetables may provide more ascorbic acid (and vitamin A) than freshly harvested snap beans, head lettuce, or even tomatoes.

Cabbage is a more stable source of ascorbic acid than most leafy vegetables, so plan to use the more perishable ones first and store the cabbage for later use. Even if you hold it at room temperature (between 65° and 80° F.) for a few days, cabbage, unlike most vegetables, will hold its ascorbic acid well. However, if you keep cabbage in cold storage under 40° F., it will retain as much as three fourths or more of its ascorbic acid for at least two months. Remember not to allow cabbages to dry out in storage. Keep them moist by wrapping them in damp towels and store them in the vegetable crisper of the refrigerator, where the humidity is high.

Peppers, snap beans, lima beans and tomatoes are all vegetables that retain their ascorbic acid well at room temperature. Originally they were tropical plants. Unlike cabbage, they do not require high humidity.

The levels of ascorbic acid in tomatoes vary considerably. Some of the factors that produce these variations are beyond your control, being a result of plant varieties and of farming practices. But some factors that determine the levels of ascorbic acid in tomatoes are ones you can control, both in purchase and storage of tomatoes.

The ascorbic acid in tomatoes grown out-of-doors and allowed to vine-ripen in summer sunlight may be twice that of wintertime greenhouse-grown tomatoes. Green tomatoes, just beginning to turn color, become a good source of ascorbic acid if you allow them full exposure to sunlight. Such tomatoes can develop more ascorbic acid than tomatoes from the same plant ripened under foliage. There are also regional variations. If you have a choice, remember that tomatoes produced on the West Coast are apt to have higher levels of ascorbic acid (and vitamin A) than tomatoes grown in the Midwest.

Tomatoes picked before they redden fail to reach their best appearance or nutritive value if you put them on a hot windowsill or in the refrigerator. A bright-red color fails to develop if the temperature rises above 85° F. and stays there for long stretches of time. To redden tomatoes, store them between 60° and 75° F.

Tomatoes ripened in the refrigerator are apt to become soft and watery, and they decay readily.

If you hold firm, ripe tomatoes at room temperature for several days, or even up to a week, they will retain their ascorbic acid. But if you do this with overripe tomatoes, they lose their ascorbic acid rapidly.

Carrots, white and sweet potatoes, and other roots and tubers will retain their most important nutrients reasonably well if you store them outside of the refrigerator. But you must keep them cool and moist enough to prevent them from withering. They spoil quickly if they are in direct contact with water, so don't allow condensation moisture to form on them. If you live in the suburbs or country, keep root and tuberous vegetables in a root cellar, a well-ventilated cool basement, an unheated pantry, or a garage. If you are an urban dweller, buy such vegetables in small quantities and store them briefly if you need to store them at kitchen temperature.

Some vegetables are rich sources of carotene, as well as ascorbic acid. Beta carotene is often called pro-vitamin A, for it can be converted by the human body to vitamin A. For this reason, "vitamin A value" may refer either to vitamin A itself or to one of its precursors such as beta carotene. Carrots and sweet potatoes are unique among roots and tubers for their high carotene content. Carotene is considered the carrot's most important nutrient. Removing the carrot tops does not affect the vitamin A value.

Sweet potatoes, especially deep-orange varieties, are important sources of carotene. Right after sweet potatoes are harvested their carotene content is high. But unlike most vegetables, their carotene content usually *increases* during the storage period before sweet potatoes reach retail markets. After about six months, the carotene content begins to drop, but sweet potatoes are not usually stored longer than six months.

If you notice sweet potatoes developing any mold, discard them. Certain types of mold on sweet potatoes are toxic.

Potatoes, parsnips, turnips and sweet potatoes are not considered exceptionally good sources of ascorbic acid, but they do contribute fair amounts of this vitamin to the daily diet. Ascorbic acid is highest in potatoes when they are freshly dug. Immature potatoes contain more ascorbic acid than potatoes left in the ground to mature. Stored potatoes suffer a progressive loss of ascorbic acid. The loss occurs most rapidly during the early weeks of storage. After roughly three months of storage, potatoes retain approximately half their original ascorbic acid supply; after six months, only one third.

If you store potatoes for a long time at temperatures a few degrees above freezing they may develop an undesirable sweet flavor. Such chilling does not spoil their nutrient content. The bland flavor of the potatoes will return if you place them at room temperature for a few days.

Always store potatoes in the dark. If you buy them in brown bags that contain air holes, these bags make good storage containers for the potatoes at home. If you store potatoes in the light, they develop poisonous green skins. Discard such potatoes, or at least remove all of the green portions. Never eat potato sprouts; they are poisonous. Discard any blighted potatoes. Some naturally occurring chemicals present in blighted potatoes, or possibly some compounds which are as yet unidentified but suspected of being toxic, may be hazardous to human health.

Sweet potatoes, like white potatoes, lose a great amount of ascorbic acid during early months of storage, followed by a more gradual loss. At the end of three months—at which time three fourths of the sweet-potato crop has probably reached consumers —some 30 to 40 percent of the original ascorbic content may be lost; in six months, another 10 percent. As mentioned earlier, sweet potatoes are usually not stored for longer than six months.

Storing Frozen Vegetables

If you buy commercially frozen vegetables, transfer them to your home freezer, or at least to the freezing compartment of your refrigerator, as soon as you arrive home. Never thaw and then refreeze vegetables. Both their flavor and ascorbic acid content will decline.

Hold frozen vegetables well below freezing to preserve their ascorbic acid level. If you hold them merely at the freezing point, they will show progressive loss of ascorbic acid. The freezing compartment of a home refrigerator is suitable for storing frozen vegetables only for very brief periods.

The recommended maximum storage period for home-frozen vegetables in a home freezer kept at 0° F. is from 8 to 12 months. At 0° F., frozen beans, broccoli, cauliflower and spinach will lose one third to three fourths of their ascorbic acid within a year. If you can store them as low as —20° F. such vegetables will hold far more of their ascorbic acid. Unfortunately, most home freezers are not constructed to operate at such a low temperature. If you are unable to maintain your freezer well below 0° F. buy frozen vegetables in small quantities and replenish the supply frequently.

If you freeze home-grown vegetables, naturally you will wish to stock a large supply in the freezer in order to enjoy them for many months—perhaps for an entire year. Although their ascorbic acid content will decline, other nutrients will be retained.

According to the "experts," tomatoes do not freeze well. They are not frozen commercially. However, Ruth Stout, that incomparable gardener, has been freezing tomatoes successfully for years. She suggests that tomatoes be cut into wedges, unpeeled and raw, and placed in containers for freezing. These tomatoes, when thawed, can be used for salad, even though they will no longer be as firm as fresh ones. They can also be used for soups, stews and casseroles. Such tomatoes will have far more flavor than most reaching Northern markets during the winter and spring months.

Preparing Fresh Vegetables for Cooking

Although you can eat many vegetables raw, certain ones *should* be cooked. Cooking improves the palatability of some and the digestibility of others, especially if they are fibrous. Cooking is sometimes a safeguard against disease-producing pathogens which may contaminate crops grown with raw, uncomposted fertilizers. Certain vegetables, such as peas, beans and other legumes, should always be eaten cooked. They contain naturally occurring toxic substances which are deactivated by heat.

The degree to which precious nutrients are saved or lost will depend upon the manner in which you prepare and clean vegetables before you cook them. Naturally, you will need to do some peeling, trimming, scraping, rinsing and cleansing to remove damaged leaves, bruised spots, skins, dirt, insects, slugs or inedible parts. All of these operations unfortunately destroy some nutrients. Learn to minimize losses.

Currently, you face a special problem in the kitchen. You have been told repeatedly that valuable nutrients are present in the skins or just under the skins of many vegetables and fruits. But today, commercially grown produce may contain residues of pesticides, fungicides, waxes, mineral oil, anti-sprouting compounds, or even dyes—for instance in the case of sweet potatoes made to look like more expensive yams, or white potatoes made to look like more expensive new red potatoes. Is it better to leave the vegetables unpeeled but possibly containing some of these undesirable and toxic substances, or to peel them and lose precious nutrients? You will have to weigh the evidence before coming to a decision. There is no clear-cut answer to this question. The answer seems to be one of many "trade-offs." Although pesticide residue may be concentrated in the peel, it may also be present throughout the edible pulp of the produce.

Don't peel vegetables *unnecessarily*. For example, instead of peeling, just scrub the skins of white or sweet potatoes or carrots with a stiff brush. Peeled potatoes lose a little riboflavin; peeled carrots, niacin. There is more ascorbic acid in the peel and just under the skin of tomatoes than in the pulp, so leave the skins intact.

Remember that the dark outer leaves of vegetables often contain more nutrients than the pale inner ones. Alas, they also may contain greater amounts of pesticide residue. If you do decide to use them, for example, when you prepare cabbage, save the coarse outer leaves for soup or stuffed cabbage.

STUFFED CABBAGE LEAVES

12 outer cabbage leaves
water or soup stock
1½ pounds lean raw beef or lamb, chopped
1 onion, chopped fine
1 cup brown rice or buckwheat, cooked
1 tablespoon parsley, minced

Simmer the cabbage leaves in water or soup stock until the leaves are pliable. Drain and cool them. Prepare a mixture of the remaining ingredients. Place a portion of the mixture in the center of each cabbage leaf and roll it up tightly. Arrange the leaves at the bottom of a pot. Pour a small amount of the liquid over the stuffed leaves. Cover the pot and simmer for 15 minutes. Serve with a tossed salad. Serves 6.

The crisp cabbage core is rich in ascorbic acid. Dice and add it to salad.

The outer green leaves of lettuce may be coarser than the inner tender ones, but they are higher in calcium, iron and vitamin A. Use them with green peas.

GREEN PEAS AND LETTUCE

1 cup water or soup stock
4 outer lettuce leaves
3 cups green peas, raw
1 onion, chopped fine
1 teaspoon fresh mint leaves, minced, or a larger quantity of dried mint leaves, crushed*

Bring liquid to boil in a pot. Insert a steamer (see Appendix on page 205) and line it with 2 large lettuce leaves. Fill them with peas. Arrange onion and mint on top. Cover with 2 additional leaves. Cover the pot tightly and bring the liquid to a boil. Cook briefly only until the peas are tender but still retain their bright-green color. Serve the peas with the lettuce and flavorings. Serves 6.

Broccoli leaves have much higher vitamin A value than the commonly used portions of stalks and flower buds. Cook tender broccoli leaves along with the stalks and buds.

Avoid long soaking when you rinse and cleanse vegetables. Precious water-soluble nutrients, washed out of the vegetables, are lost down the sink.

* Use dried herbs in larger quantities than fresh. Crush the leaves.

The manner in which you cut vegetables will determine whether or not you preserve their nutrients. Changes in levels of ascorbic acid in cabbage, caused by different cutting practices, were investigated. Cutting was done by shredding, chopping by machine, chopping in wooden bowls, and shredding with coleslaw cutters. Losses of ascorbic acid ranged from 9 to 15 percent, with the greatest loss inflicted by shredding; the least, by machine chopping.

Cabbage kept the most ascorbic acid when it was cut with a sharp knife on a cutting board rather than with dull tools on other surfaces. Remember this when you trim, cut or shred. Use a sharp-bladed knife to prevent bruising of vegetables. Both vitamins A and C are lost whenever vegetable tissues are bruised.

Cut or shred vegetables coarsely, and do it as late as you can before you cook them. If you allow cut or shredded vegetables to be exposed to the air for any length of time, they lose nutrients through oxidation. The finer you cut or shred vegetables, the more nutrients will be extracted from them and go into the cooking liquid. This is not serious if you plan to use the liquid as well as the vegetable. It is better to cut large vegetables, such as broccoli, before you cook them, than to attempt to cook them whole. Any destructive effect due to extra surface exposure is offset, at least in part, by shortened cooking time.

Cooking Fresh Vegetables

Ascorbic acid, other vitamins and some minerals are watersoluble. To conserve these nutrients, remember the three R's of REDUCE TO A MINIMUM:

(1) the amount of liquid in which you cook vegetables;
(2) the cooking time; and
(3) the surface of the vegetable exposed.

Of these three factors, the volume of liquid in which you cook vegetables is probably the most crucial. If you cook vegetables in large quantities of liquid, you will lose more nutrients through solubility than if you keep the volume small. For example, if you cook cabbage quickly, in about one third as much volume of water as cabbage, the cabbage will retain nearly 90 percent of its ascorbic acid; in four times as much water as cabbage, less than 50 percent. Similarly, if you cook broccoli briefly in a small amount of water, it will lose only half as much ascorbic acid as if you cook it in a large quantity of water.

When you overcook vegetables, you destroy many nutrients. Color, texture and flavor are also destroyed.

If you prepare a vegetable by putting it into cold liquid, you will lose a substantial amount of ascorbic acid before the liquid begins to heat. This loss is due to enzyme activity, which probably increases during the first part of the heating period and then stops when the heat reaches a certain temperature, below boiling, at which time the enzymes are destroyed. You can shorten this critical period, as well as the total cooking time, if you allow the liquid to boil *before* you add the vegetable. Remember that rapidly boiling liquid will not cook vegetables more quickly than slowly boiling water. The highest temperature under atmospheric pressure is 212° F., which is the boiling point of water at sea level.

Boil root or tuberous vegetables in their skins, and they will retain more vitamins and minerals than if you cook them pared and cut. Tests show that potatoes boiled in their skins retain practically all of their ascorbic acid, thiamine and other nutrients. Cook beets in their skins and then peel them. You will prevent excessive loss of color and nutrients.

Your choice of cooking pots is important in order to retain nutrients as much as possible in cooked vegetables. Experimentally, cabbage was cooked in open kettles, tightly closed kettles, pressure saucepans and steamers. Then the ascorbic acid content of the cooked cabbages was measured. There was considerable variation, depending on the type of cooking pot. The most ascorbic acid was retained by using the tightly closed kettles; the least, with the open kettles. So, use pots with tightly fitted lids to cook vegetables and to prevent the escape of steam and vapor. This practice will allow you to cook vegetables in small quantities of liquid, since the liquid will not evaporate into the air.

So-called "waterless" cooking is a method of cooking vegetables with any water that may remain on them after they are rinsed, plus the juice extracted from them during cooking. Pots for this kind of cooking are usually quite expensive. You may decide that such an investment is unwarranted. "Waterless" cooking does *not* permit you to cook briefly. For this reason, you would probably not conserve the nutritive values any more significantly with such pots than if you cook vegetables briefly in small amounts of liquid using traditional pots with tight-fitting lids.

In addition to boiling vegetables, you have other cooking methods from which to choose. To conserve the nutrients, bake whole white or sweet potatoes in their skins. Baking is a satisfactory cooking method with other vegetables that require long cooking, such as acorn squash. You can bake carrots, onions, turnips, young beets, parsnips and cucumbers successfully in covered casseroles in a moderate oven (350° to 400° F.), which allows for a gradual heat penetration. For some vegetables, baking would cause considerable nutritive destruction.

You can bake some vegetables, such as eggplant, which are traditionally fried.

BAKED EGGPLANT

2 large eggplants, whole
¼ cup vegetable oil
1 teaspoon fresh basil, minced, or a larger quantity of dried basil, crushed
½ pound sharp Cheddar cheese, sliced

Wash eggplants, but keep the skins intact. Slice them into rounds, ¾ inch thick. Brush both sides with oil and arrange the rounds on shallow pans in single layers. Top them with basil and cheese. Bake uncovered for 20 minutes in a moderate oven (350° F.) until the cheese is golden brown and the eggplant slices are cooked. Do *not* turn them. Remove the rounds with a spatula, and serve them immediately, with a tossed salad. By keeping the skins on the eggplant during baking, the slices will hold together well. Serves 6.

By braising or panning vegetables, you can conserve nutrients in such succulent ones as cabbage, summer squash, kale or collards. Use a skillet, with a small amount of vegetable oil. Add the vegetable, cover the pot tightly and cook briefly.

If you use a pressure cooker for vegetables, make certain to time your cooking precisely. Improper, prolonged cooking under pressure results in unnecessary nutrient losses.

A good method for cooking many vegetables is to steam them briefly in a small amount of liquid using a special steaming device. Such steamers, made specifically for this purpose, will fit into any size pot. I suggest that before you buy a steamer, do some comparative shopping since prices often vary with no reflection on quality. (See Appendix)

Regardless of which method you choose for cooking vegetables, plan to save the cooking liquid (also called pot liquor or vegetable stock). Much of the ascorbic acid, as well as other water-soluble nutrients, lost to the vegetable can be recovered in this liquid. *Do not pour it down the sink!* Plan to serve it with the vegetable. Or, if you make a vegetable sauce, use this liquid in the sauce. Or drink it. Add it to tomato juice or to soup. Use it as part of the liquid needed for cooking rice and other grains, hot cereal or bread. If you serve this liquid at a later time it will still contribute minerals, even though some of the ascorbic acid and thiamine will be destroyed by its standing and being reheated.

The point cannot be emphasized too strongly that severe losses of nutrients can occur in the kitchen from methods of vegetable storage, preparation and cooking, heaped on those already inflicted by shipments from long distances and by supermarket storage. As someone aptly phrased the problem, a great deal happens to nutrients "between garden and gullet."

The USDA investigated these problems of nutrient losses in vegetables due to food preparation and cooking. With certain kitchen practices, leafy green vegetables and yellow ones lost as much as 45 percent thiamine, 40 percent of riboflavin and of niacin, and 50 percent ascorbic acid. Other vegetables lost 20 percent each of thiamine, riboflavin and niacin, and 25 percent ascorbic acid.

How you handle vegetables *after* you cook them becomes another matter for concern. For example, if you allow *steamed* potatoes in their skins to stand for as long as a half hour, they will not suffer any loss of ascorbic acid. But in the same amount of time, *baked* potatoes in their skins, as well as French fried potatoes, may have lost as much as 34 percent of their ascorbic acid. If you have peeled, cut and then baked the potatoes, they may have lost as much as 48 percent. If you have spent time to peel, cut in half, steam and then mash and cream them, they may have lost 63 percent. And, if you have been imprudent enough to peel, cut and soak the potatoes in water for two hours to keep them white, and then bake them, they may have lost 76 percent. Whenever cooked potatoes are allowed to stand for long periods, as they frequently do on restaurant steam tables, the ascorbic acid loss progresses rapidly. After 1¼ hours of standing, potatoes that have been peeled, cut in half, steamed, mashed and creamed may have lost as much as 95 percent of their ascorbic acid. The moral of this experiment is to save you time and effort as well as nutrients. Cook vegetables briefly, serve them promptly, and refrain from mashing or other forms of mauling them.

Factors such as color, texture and flavor of vegetables are closely related to cooking procedure. Overcooked vegetables are less palatable than crisp ones. Most vegetables have a mild sweet flavor when they are briefly cooked; when overcooked they develop strong, unpleasant flavors.

The attractive bright colors of vegetables can be kept if you cook briefly. Green vegetables such as spinach, chard, green snap beans, peas, broccoli and green cabbage, when cooked only to a crisp stage, will retain their color. This is a far better procedure than resorting to a vitamin destroyer such as bicarbonate of soda to give overcooked vegetables a cosmetic uplift.

If you live in an area where the water is hard (alkaline), brief cooking of vegetables will help to keep them green. Hard water turns cooked red cabbage into hues of violet or blue. It will turn the white color of potatoes, cauliflower, white cabbage, celery, turnips and white onions into shades of yellow when you cook them. If you would like to have these vegetables retain their whiteness, add a teaspoonful of lemon juice to the cooking water. Use fresh lemon juice, not the reconstituted type, which contains an objectionable and toxic preservative.

Fortunately, yellow vegetables such as carrots, corn, squash, pumpkin and rutabaga keep their attractive color well during cooking, since their yellow color is heat-stabile.

Cooking Frozen Vegetables

Cook a frozen vegetable *unthawed* in a small amount of boiling liquid, in a tightly covered pot. After the vegetable is added, bring the liquid back to a boil quickly over high heat. Then use low heat to maintain gentle boiling. Cook the vegetable only long enough to make it crisp and tender. Do not overcook.

Dressing Up Cooked Vegetables

If you have cooked vegetables with tender loving care, they will be good eating *au naturel*. If you are accustomed to topping vegetables with butter or cream sauce, for variety try lemon juice, yogurt, sour cream, or tahini (sesame butter) instead. As garnishes for vegetable dishes, try minced chive or parsley, slivered almonds, toasted soybeans, wheat germ, grated sharp cheese or unsweetened dry coconut shreds.

Herbs and other seasonings are especially good to dress up cooked vegetables. Cook them with the vegetables, tie them in a small retrievable bag, put them in the steaming liquid of the steamer or add them to the cooked vegetables just before you serve them. If you are a novice in using herbs or other seasonings, there are no rigid rules. Try new flavorings sparingly and experiment until you discover what you enjoy most. The following are merely suggestions.

Artichoke, French or globe: basil, bay leaf, fennel, garlic or oregano

Artichoke, Jerusalem: nutmeg or tarragon

Asparagus: allspice, cardamom, coriander, nutmeg, rosemary, sesame or tarragon

Beans, lima: chive, dill, marjoram, oregano, parsley, sage, savory, tarragon or thyme

Beans, snap or wax: basil, caraway, chive, coriander, dill, garlic, marjoram, mint, oregano, savory, tarragon or thyme

Beets: allspice, bay leaves, caraway, celery seeds, cinnamon, clove, cumin, dill, ginger, nutmeg, savory or thyme

Broccoli: caraway, dill or tarragon

Brussels sprouts: basil, caraway, dill, nutmeg, sage or thyme

Cabbage, green: basil, caraway, celery seeds, cumin, dill, fennel, mint, nutmeg, savory or tarragon

Cabbage, red: allspice, basil, caraway, celery seeds, cinnamon, clove, cumin, dill, mint, nutmeg, savory or tarragon

Cardoon: clove, garlic or parsley

Carrots: allspice, basil, bay leaves, caraway, clove, dill, fennel seeds, ginger, mace, marjoram, mint, nutmeg, poppy seeds, sage or thyme

Cauliflower: caraway, celery seeds, chive, clove, dill, mace, nutmeg, paprika, poppy seeds, rosemary, tarragon or thyme

Celeriac: basil, chive, dill or tarragon

Celery: basil, chive, dill or tarragon

Corn: basil, chive, oregano or garlic

Eggplant: basil, garlic, marjoram, oregano or sage

Fennel: parsley

Greens: allspice, coriander, mace, nutmeg or rosemary

Kohlrabi: tarragon or thyme

Leeks: basil, ginger, rosemary, sage or thyme

Okra: chive, paprika or thyme

Onions: basil, caraway, nutmeg, oregano, sage or thyme

Parsnips: cinnamon, ginger, tarragon or thyme

Peas, green: basil, chive, dill, marjoram, mint, nutmeg, oregano, poppy seed, rosemary, savory, tarragon or thyme

Potatoes, sweet: allspice, cardamom, cinnamon, clove or nutmeg

Potatoes, white: caraway, celery seeds, chive, dill, paprika, parsley or rosemary

Rappini: caraway, dill or tarragon

Rutabaga: bay leaves, cardamom, clove or mint

Spinach: basil, mace, marjoram, nutmeg, oregano or sesame

Squash, summer: basil, chive, dill, marjoram, nutmeg, oregano, rosemary or thyme

Squash, winter: allspice, cinnamon, clove, nutmeg or mace

Tomatoes: basil, bay leaves, celery seed, clove, dill, oregano, sage, sesame, tarragon or thyme

Turnip, white: bay leaves, cardamom, clove or mint

Lively Leftovers

To save time, some busy individuals cook enough vegetables for two meal servings. This saving of time is done at the expense of nutrients. Whenever you hold and reheat cooked vegetables they suffer losses, especially of ascorbic acid.

Plan to prepare only enough of a vegetable for one meal and avoid needless leftovers. At times, of course, we all have leftovers. Do we face them as problems or challenges?

The longer you store cooked vegetables, the greater the ascorbic acid loss. After cooked vegetables have been in your refrigerator for one day, they will have only about three fourths as much ascorbic acid as when you first cooked them; after two days, only about two thirds. If you reheat cooked vegetables after having held them for two or three days in the refrigerator, they will have only a third or a half as much ascorbic acid as when you first cooked them.

You can minimize these losses. Refrigerate any leftover cooked vegetables promptly as soon as they are cool and plan to use them within a day or two, *without reheating*. There are many dishes that you can create with cold cooked vegetables. Drain off the juices and use the juices as suggested on page 35. Below are a few suggestions for lively leftover dishes. Hopefully, they will suggest others to you, drawn from your own creative talents.

VEGETABLE MÉLANGE

2 cups cooked vegetables (carrots, peas, onions, string beans, etc.)
1 cup raw vegetables (diced celery, green peppers, etc.)
¼ cup yogurt or sour cream
   herbs and seasonings
¼ cup pimento, diced
   bed of crisp lettuce

Drain off all the juices from the cooked vegetables and reserve them for other uses. Mix together the cooked and raw vegetables, moisten with yogurt or sour cream, add herbs and seasonings, and garnish with pimento on a bed of lettuce. Chill. Serves 6.

VEGETABLE ASPIC

1 tablespoon unflavored gelatin
2 cups tomato juice
1 teaspoon fresh tarragon, minced or a larger quantity of dried tarragon, crushed
1 cup mixed cooked vegetables
½ cup mixed raw vegetables (diced carrots, radishes, etc.)

Soften the gelatin in ½ cup of cold tomato juice. Heat the remaining juice, with the tarragon, to the simmer point. Remove the mixture from the heat and dissolve the gelatin mixture in it. Allow this mixture to cool for 10 minutes. Add the remaining ingredients. Mix well and turn into a rinsed mold or 6 individual custard cups. Chill until the gelatin is firm. Unmold. Serves 6.

SAVORY STRING BEANS

2 cups string beans or wax beans, cooked
¼ cup apple-cider vinegar
½ cup vegetable oil
¼ teaspoon fresh summer savory, minced, or a larger quantity of
    dried summer savory, crushed
¼ cup pimento, diced

Marinate the beans in vinegar and oil, with summer savory. Garnish with pimento. Chill. This dish is a good accompaniment to cold roast beef, lamb or chicken. Serves 6.

ASPARAGUS SALAD

bed of salad greens
12 spears of asparagus, cooked
2 red or green peppers, sliced in rings
½ cup yogurt or sour cream
1 tablespoon chives, minced
½ teaspoon curry powder

Arrange salad greens on platter. Place asparagus spears and pepper rings on top. Mix yogurt or sour cream with chives and curry, and add this as a topping. Chill. Serves 6.

Cabbage, sweet and sour, is a traditional dish. I have adapted it, with briefer cooking time, and enjoy it as a hot cooked vegetable. However, the leftover cabbage, when served cold, is equally delicious.

CABBAGE, SWEET AND SOUR

4 cups cabbage (red or green), cut coarsely
1 onion, sliced
¼ cup apple-cider vinegar
2 tart apples, with skins, diced
2 tablespoons honey
½ cup raisins
1 tablespoon caraway seeds
¼ cup vegetable oil
2 stalks celery with leaves, diced

Blend all ingredients together in a large pot. Cover the pot tightly and cook over fairly high heat for 5 minutes. Serve immediately. Serves 6, with possible leftovers. Serve cold the following day.

COLD BEET SOUP (BORSCHT)

2 cups beets, cooked
2 cups liquid in which beets were cooked
    juice of 1 lemon
1 onion, raw
    seasoning
½ cup yogurt or sour cream

Blend all ingredients together in an electric blender until the mixture is smooth. Chill. Serves 6.

The next time you open your refrigerator, discover what cold cooked vegetables you can combine to create appetizing dishes.

Suggested Reading

Bring, S. V., Grassl, C., Hofstrand, J. T., & Willard, M. J., "Total Ascorbic Acid in Potatoes." *Journal of the American Dietetic Association,* Vol. 42, No. 4, April 1963, pp. 320–24.

Bring, S. V. & Raab, F. P., "Total Ascorbic Acid in Potatoes." *Journal of the American Dietetic Association,* Vol. 45, No. 2, August 1964, pp. 149–52.

Kahn, R. M. & Halliday, E. G., "Ascorbic Acid Content of White Potatoes as Affected by Cooking and Standing on Steam Table." *Journal of the American Dietetic Association,* Vol. 20, No. 4, April 1944, pp. 220–22.

Leichsenring, J. M., Pilcher, H. L., & Norris, L. M., II "Effect of Baking and of Pressure-cooking on the Ascorbic Dehydroascorbic and Diketogulonic Acid Contents of Potatoes." *Food Research,* Vol. 22, No. 1, January-February 1957, pp. 44–50.

Mayer, Jean, "Canned, Fresh or Frozen?" *Family Health,* Vol. 4, No. 5, May 1972, pp. 26–29.

Patten, M. B. & Green, M. E. "Cabbage, Factors Affecting Vitamin Values and Palatability." Wooster, Ohio: Ohio Agricultural Experiment Station, Bulletin No. 742, April 1954.

Quat, Helen, *The Wonderful World of Freezer Cooking.* New York: Hearthside Press, 1964, pp. 125–42.

Schroeder, Henry A., "Losses of Vitamins and Trace Minerals Resulting from Processing and Preservation of Foods." *American Journal of Clinical Nutrition,* Vol. 24, May 1971, pp. 562–73.

Tucker, R. E., Brown, P. T., & Hedrick, D., *Ascorbic Acid Content of Fruits and Vegetables Served College Students.* Kingston, Rhode Island: Rhode Island Agricultural Experiment Station, Bulletin No. 331, 1955.

USDA publications:

Conserving the Nutritive Values in Foods, G90, 1971.

Food, Yearbook, 1959.

Food and Life, Yearbook, 1939.

Food for Us All, Yearbook, 1969.

Green Vegetables for Good Eating, Home & Garden Bulletin No. 41, May 1959.

Home Canning of Fruits and Vegetables, G8, 1972.

Home Freezing of Fruits and Vegetables, G10, 1971.

Storing Perishable Foods in the Home, G78, 1971.

Storing Vegetables and Fruits in Basements, Cellars, Outbuildings and Pits, G119, 1970.

Vegetables in Family Meals, A Guide for Consumers, G105, 1971.

Your Money's Worth in Foods, Home & Garden Bulletin No. 183, December 1970.

Vegetables in Family Meals, A Guide for Consumers, G105, 1971

2 Perking Up the Salad Bowl

✲

You can add many good ingredients to the salad to give a variety of colors, flavors and textures. Salads are important sources for vitamins and minerals, and their cellulose content is important for bulk. Use salads as appetizers, as accompaniments to entrées, as desserts, and as meals in themselves. Usually salads are served crisp and cold. You can make them plain or fancy, savory or sweet, and you can combine different ingredients in almost endless ways.

Shopping for Salad Greens

Look for greens that are fresh, crisp and deep green in color. Limp greens or those with yellowing leaves are apt to be past their prime, tough and bitter. For the best nutritional buys, shop for head lettuce or cabbage that still have lots of outer leaves; reject the well-trimmed heads. The outer leaves of lettuce, cabbage and other greens are loaded with carotene, while the inner leaves have almost none.

Both the intensity of the vegetable's greenness and the part of the plant from which it comes are clues to its food value. Generally, the greener the vegetable, the richer it is in vitamins and minerals. Be guided by this rule in choosing, for example, dark-green pascal celery rather than blanched stalks. Dark-green leaves may carry several times as much of some nutrients as that contained in their stalks. So, plan also to use the leaves of celery as well as the stalks. Many of the most nutritious salad greens are slightly bitter but pleasant-tasting, especially if you serve them with a good dressing.

Expand the variety of greens you commonly choose. If you have a vegetable garden, you can buy seeds for many delicious types of salad greens that are rarely grown commercially because they are too tender or perishable to ship or store well. Occasionally you may be fortunate in finding some "native" produce sold as local surplus, or to locate some at a bona fide "truck farm" roadside market. The types of salad greens found in different sections of the country vary; be adventurous and willing to try the specialties of your region.

The following are those usually found in most places, in season.

Beet greens: These are sometimes sold separately, especially when young beet plants are thinned out early in the growing season. The young, tender beet greens can be used in salad. At times the greens are still attached to the tops of beets, although this practice is fast disappearing. If the greens are still crisp and fresh, use the tender ones for salad, and the larger, coarser ones as cooked greens.

Cabbage, Chinese, or *Celery cabbage:* Use this crisp cabbage, with its slight anise flavor, like other cabbage in salad. Choose solid heads with medium-green color.

Cabbage, green or *Cabbage, white:* Use cabbage as a salad base or an ingredient of salad. Cole slaw, of course, is a familiar item.

Cabbage, red: This variety is interchangeable with green cabbage. Red cabbage is slightly higher in some nutrients than the green cabbage.

Cabbage, savoy: Although this crinkly variety of cabbage, bright green, with a tangy mustard flavor, is usually cooked, a small amount of it is good raw in a mixed green salad.

Celery: Stalks and leaves should have a crisp, fresh look. Avoid wilted or blanched stalks.

Chard, Swiss: Use only the young, tender leaves, without midribs, in salad; cook the coarse ones.

Chicory or *Curly endive:* The lacy leaves spread out, dark green at the outside to yellow at the center. The entire head of chicory, with its slightly bitter taste, mixes well with other salad greens. If the outer leaves are very large and bitter, use them as a cooked vegetable.

Dandelion leaves: Two varieties reach the market in spring. One is cultivated, with long, pale-green leaves and a mild flavor; the other is field grown, with shorter, darker leaves and more bitterness. Reject any dandelion leaves if they are already blossoming. At this stage they are unduly bitter. Dandelion leaves mix well with other salad greens, or they can be cooked as a vegetable.

Endive, Belgian, or *Endive, French:* This long, narrow, very pale yellow and firm headed green has tightly packed, wide, pointed waxy leaves. Belgian endive has an unusually tangy flavor, and its light color forms a contrast to deeply colored leaves in a mixed green salad.

Escarole: This salad green is distinguished by its dark-green non-curly leaves. The outer leaves may be bitter, in which case you can cook them as a vegetable. Use the less bitter inner leaves for salad.

Fennel or *Finocchio* or *Anise:* As mentioned earlier (see pages 14–15) this pearly-white bulb has bright, featherlike green leaves and a mild licorice flavor. Use fennel in mixed salad or cook it as a vegetable.

Field salad or *Field lettuce* or *Lamb's tongue:* This is a salad green that appears infrequently on the market. It consists of very small spears on delicate stems. If you are fortunate enough to find it, try it in a mixed green salad.

Kale: Small amounts of this highly nutritious crinkly green, with midribs removed, can be minced into a mixed salad. The mature outer leaves are apt to be tough, even when cooked. I learned this fact by experience. On one occasion I saw kale used in a butcher shop during the wintertime as trimming on the meat trays. Kale was not being sold in vegetable stores at the time. I asked the butcher if he would sell me some of his trimming. He looked at me in puzzlement but agreed to sell it. Upon cooking the kale, I understood the butcher's expression. The kale was disappointingly tough and exceedingly bitter. Apparently the outer leaves were discards from someone's garden, since kale flourishes even when snow covers the ground. This incident taught me to use only tender young kale leaves.

Lettuce: Five types of lettuce have been developed: looseleaf or nonheading; butterhead, with soft leaves grown in a closed head; cabbagehead, with closed head of crisp leaves; cos or romaine, with tall or elongated head; and stem lettuce or celtuce, grown for the thick stem rather than the leaves. Of the five types, head lettuce is most popular.

Lettuce, Bibb: This miniature, fragile head is considered by many individuals to be the choicest of lettuce. Each leaf shades from green at the edge to yellow toward the center. It is grown in limestone soil, and is sometimes called limestone lettuce. Unfortunately, Bibb lettuce is not always available, and when it is, it is often expensive.

Lettuce, Boston: This is one of the common varieties of head lettuce. It has a dark-green, loosely formed head. Select a quality head in medium weight for its size. If you squeeze it gently, the head should "give" slightly. Look for outside leaves that are fresh and green and separate easily.

Lettuce, iceberg: This is another common variety of head lettuce. It is pale green and watery, with a compact head. It has a very bland flavor. During the summertime, bright-green, scarcely formed heads of iceberg lettuce may reach stores from nearby sources. When you shop for iceberg lettuce, look for features similar to those of Boston lettuce.

Lettuce, leaf: This type of lettuce is generally grown in a home garden. The leaves are soft, long, tender, fragile and flavorsome. Alas, it neither keeps nor ships well. If you have your own vegetable garden, among many delicious varieties that you can grow are oak leaf, salad bowl, Simpson lettuce, and the seldom-planted stem lettuce.

Lettuce, romaine or *Lettuce, cos:* This lettuce, with its long, narrow head and oval leaves that are dark green outside and yellow at the heart, is a crisp, juicy, firm yet tasty lettuce. It stores well. Select romaine lettuce with fresh-looking crisp leaves which have a minimum of blemishes. The outer leaves may be coarse, with heavy midribs. Shred such leaves for salad or cook them as greens.

Mustard greens: As mentioned earlier (see page 15) you should select fresh, green, tender leaves with a bright-green color and a minimum of yellowed leaves. Reject any mustard greens that are already blossoming. Add a few of the tender leaves to salad and cook the remainder as a vegetable.

Parsley: Although most people use flat-leaf or curly-leaf parsley sparingly as garnishes, both varieties can be used in great quantities in salad. Parsley is highly nutritious as well as tangy. Select bunches that are deep green and crisp.

Spinach: Raw spinach, with its rich, deep-green color, gives a good color contrast with other greens in a mixed salad. When you coat raw spinach leaves with salad dressing, it is difficult to recognize the "spinach" flavor. Select crisp fresh leaves and use the tender ones, without stems or midribs, for salad.

Turnip greens: These are sometimes sold separately from their white roots, as another cooking vegetable. When the leaves are young, fresh and tender, add them to salad.

Watercress: This is a pungent salad green, sold in small bunches, with many small, round, dark green leaves. Watercress gives a lively flavor to a mixed salad. Select bunches with bright, deep-green crisp leaves.

If you have your own vegetable garden, you can grow some salad greens that are not sold in stores. These include the young leaves of comfrey, garden cress, peppergrass and nasturtium leaves.

If you search among weeds of wayside and field, you will find many kinds of leaves that you can add to a salad. Some are lamb's quarter, purslane, shepherd's purse, wild chicory and wild dandelion leaves.

A Cautionary Note on Choosing Salad Greens

Never use rhubarb leaves, either raw in salad or cooked. Rhubarb leaves have great concentrations of oxalic acid and they are toxic. Leaves of some other edible plants used in salads or as cooked vegetables also contain oxalic acid, but in lesser quantities. These include collards, kale, mustard greens, sorrel, spinach,

Swiss chard and turnip greens. These oxalate-rich foods, used infrequently and in limited quantities, present no problem, provided that your diet is varied. But as a further precaution, when you eat foods containing oxalic acid, plan to eat calcium-rich foods at the same meal. For example, use milk or milk products such as cheese, along with oxalate-containing foods; the calcium will help buffer the effects of the oxalic acid.

Storing Salad Greens

Store lettuce, celery and other raw salad greens in the vegetable crisper of the refrigerator at about 45° F. Keep these greens moist and cool. Use salad bags to keep their moisture from evaporating.

To store parsley, wash it and shake to remove excess moisture. Put the parsley in a covered jar and refrigerate it.

Place the stems of a watercress bunch in a jar of cold water and refrigerate it. Cover the jar loosely.

Use salad greens promptly. Many of them are quite perishable.

Other Additions to the Vegetable Salad

Although greens are primarily the basis for a vegetable salad, many other raw vegetables can be added. Score yourself—from Avocado to Zucchini—using the following as a checklist.

Avocado: To hasten the ripening, place it in a closed paper bag. If you are not certain whether an avocado is ripe, cut out a thin wedge with a sharp knife. If the flesh is still hard, carefully replace the wedge and wrap the avocado in a bag to keep out air. Check it daily. When it is ripe, peel, slice or dice, and add it to salad.

Beet: A small amount of grated raw, peeled beet is especially good in salad if it is mixed with other grated root vegetables; a large amount tends to overpower with its flavor and color.

Broccoli leaves: Use young tender ones in salad.

Carrot: Scrub, slice, dice or grate carrot in salad.

Cauliflower: Slice cauliflowerettes thin for salad; use young tender leaves.

Cucumber: Peel, if the skin is waxed, and slice or dice it for salad.

Kohlrabi: Peel and grate raw kohlrabi and use the young tender leaves in salad.

Mushroom: Scrub and slice raw mushrooms thin; marinate the slices in salad dressing before adding them to the salad.

Onion: Peel and mince, grate, slice or dice various types of onion for salad.

Parsnip: A small amount of scrubbed grated raw parsnip is good in salad, especially mixed with other root vegetables.

Pepper, sweet (green or red): Use sliced or diced peppers as ingredients or garnishes for salad.

Radish: Use whole or sliced radishes as ingredients or garnishes for salads.

Scallion: Peel and slice scallions. Use crisp green tops by mincing them with a pair of kitchen shears.

Shallot: Peel and mince shallots for salad.

Tomato: Use various types of tomatoes for salad. Keep small cherry tomatoes whole, and slice or quarter larger varieties. Use yellow as well as red tomatoes.

Turnip, white purple-topped, and *Rutabaga, yellow:* Scrub and slice, dice or grate white turnips; scrub (or peel, if the skin is waxed) yellow rutabagas, then dice or grate into salad.

Zucchini: Slice raw young zucchini for salad.

Include items in the salad that in the past you thoughtlessly may have discarded: celery leaves, core of cabbage, onion sprouts and leaves of turnip tops which have been cut but have begun to sprout again.

Use herbs as salad ingredients, if they are not already part of the dressing. If you use fresh herbs such as chives or parsley, mince them with a pair of kitchen shears. Crush and marinate dried herbs in the salad dressing to bring out their flavors most effectively. Try, at different times, fresh basil, chervil, chives, dill, marjoram, mint, oregano, parsley, rosemary, sage, savory or thyme. Use them sparingly; a little goes a long way.

For variety, add whole hulled sunflower, pumpkin or sesame seeds to salads. At different times, try some crushed seeds such as anise, caraway, celery, coriander, cumin, dill, fennel or poppy.

Cleaning Salad Greens

To prepare salad greens, remove the coarse outer leaves and rinse the rest quickly but thoroughly in cold water. To separate the leaves of head lettuce, cut out the core or stem. Hold the lettuce in both hands while allowing a stream of cold water to flow forcefully into the core cavity. Then, gently loosen the leaves with your thumbs. Turn the head right side up, and allow the water to drain out. Pull the head apart and pat the leaves dry with a cloth or paper towel.

To clean romaine, escarole and other clusters of firm lettuce, first pull the leaves apart, then wash and pat them dry. Tender lettuce, such as Boston, field and others, are too delicate to be patted dry. Simply spread them out on a cloth or paper towel and air-dry them.

A French salad basket is useful for cleaning other types of salad greens. Place the greens in the basket, rinse the leaves with a steady stream of cold water and twirl the salad basket. It is important to get rid of this excess water for two reasons. If you don't, the greens will wilt. Also, wet greens tend to dilute the salad dressing. You can place the washed, drained greens in a salad bag and refrigerate them to keep them crisp until you make the salad.

Keeping the Salad Crisp

To keep salad fresh and crisp, prepare it as close as possible to serving time. Tear the salad greens into bite-size pieces, large enough to give body to the salad. Or, if you prefer, cut them with a pair of kitchen scissors. As mentioned earlier, all cutting operations of peeling, slicing, dicing and grating inflict some nutritional losses in vegetables. Whenever you can, cut vegetables coarsely. Whenever possible, keep vegetables whole, such as small cherry tomatoes or radishes.

Add dressing, especially to green salad, just before serving it. Greens, particularly lettuce, wilt quickly once dressing has been added. Use only enough dressing to moisten the salad ingredients, not so much that the leaves swim in it.

To keep alfalfa sprouts from wilting, arrange them on top of the salad, *after* you add the dressing and toss the salad.

If you use sliced tomatoes in salad, add them last. They tend to thin salad dressings.

Salads, Salads!

There are endless varieties of salad combinations. Here are a few suggestions. Create your own.

—green cabbage, onions and pimentos
—spinach, lettuce and tomatoes
—green cabbage, carrots and green peppers
—Bibb lettuce, beet greens and Spanish onions
—Chinese cabbage, parsley and sprouts
—watercress, avocado, celery and scallions
—red cabbage, apple, raisins, celery leaves and caraway seeds
—Boston lettuce, savoy cabbage, pear tomatoes, green peppers and Bermuda onions
—iceberg lettuce, sweet red peppers, chicory and chives
—Belgian endive, escarole, beefsteak tomatoes and basil
—garden lettuce, fennel and parsley
—carrots, white turnips, radishes, beets and dill
—celery stalks and leaves, fresh pineapple, sprouts and pecans
—spinach, escarole, Belgian endive and oranges
—chicory, avocado, blue cheese and shallots
—dandelion leaves, iceberg lettuce and radishes
—Boston lettuce, fennel and parsley

Double-duty Salad Preparations

When you prepare vegetables for cooking, save a few raw pieces to toss in the salad.

When you prepare vegetables for salad, cut additional ones. Store them in the refrigerator, and make them accessible as "snack food" for the whole family. Include sticks of carrot, celery and turnip; rings of green and red pepper; wheels of zucchini and cucumber. Use such finger salad as between-meal or television-watching nibbles at home, or pack them in a bag for motoring or picnicking.

Dressings: *The Salad's Crowning Glory*

Salad dressing makes an important contribution to the daily diet as a source of essential fatty acids from the oils used, as well as for the flavor and zip it gives to the salad. Although a wide range of commercial salad dressings are available, you can make your own dressings easily and inexpensively—and control the ingredients you use. Learn to make a basic dressing; then vary it as you like.

The three basic ingredients in all salad dressings are oil, vinegar (or lemon juice) and seasonings. Select these items with care, and use the best quality you can find.

Many vegetable oils can be used in salad dressing, including oil from corn, olives, peanuts, safflower, sesame seeds, soybeans and sunflower seeds. Others, encountered less frequently, include almond, avocado and walnut. Some are mild, others are strong. Experiment to find out which ones you like best. Vegetable oils are perishable. Refrigerate them once you have opened the containers.

At times, you may find different vegetable oils blended together in one product. Each oil contains different amounts of essential fatty acids. By being blended together, some of each of these valuable nutrients can be included. However, the blending of different oils may be merely a technique for producing an inferior product. An olive oil blend, for example, may be a mixture in which a small quantity of expensive olive oil is diluted with a large quantity of inexpensive oil such as cottonseed. Shun cottonseed oil or any blends of vegetable oil made with it. Although cottonseed oil is edible, cotton as a crop is subjected to extensive pesticidal spraying. Residues may be concentrated in the oil. Read labels especially carefully when you shop for vegetable oils.

Vinegar is usually a by-product of fermented beverages. Many types of vinegar are excellent for salad. Apple cider, malt and wine vinegars are perhaps the most familiar. Other vinegars include products made from grape juice, oranges, pineapple and honey.

HOMEMADE APPLE CIDER VINEGAR

Homemade vinegar is easy and inexpensive to make. The simplest method is to allow sweet cider to turn to vinegar. Allow an uncapped jug of sweet cider to stand for a few weeks in a warm room, but cover it with several layers of plastic netting or cheesecloth. After the fermentation is complete, cap the jug.

You can make apple-cider vinegar from apple wastes. Put the peelings, cores and bruised apples into a widemouthed crock. Cover the contents with cold water. Cover the crock and store it in a warm place. From time to time, add fresh peelings, cores and bruised apples. The "mother" that forms on top, a viscous, gelatinous substance, will ultimately convert the mixture to vinegar. After several months, when the vinegar in the crock tastes strong, strain, bottle and cork. Save the "mother" as a starter to hasten the fermentation in a subsequent batch.

You can make apple-cider vinegar from apples. Choose sound, tart fruit. Wash and cut unpeeled apples into small pieces, and include the cores. Put them into an electric juicer or meat grinder to obtain a mash. Strain the mash through several layers of plastic netting or cheesecloth and pour the juice into glass jugs. Cover the tops of the jugs with several layers of plastic netting or cheesecloth. Store the jugs for about 6 months in a cool, dark place. Then strain the liquid, pour it into clean jugs and cork the jugs.

In England, when beer and ale are soured, the by-product is malt vinegar. Make your own version.

HOMEMADE MALT VINEGAR

3 pounds hop-flavored malt extract
2 pounds honey
3 quarts hot water
2 gallons cold water
1 cake baking yeast (or 1 tablespoon dry yeast granules)
¼ cup warm water
3 quarts vinegar
1 pint apple juice, unpasteurized

Dissolve the malt extract and honey in the hot water. Allow the mixture to cool. Then combine it with the cold water. Pour the mixture into a 5-gallon crock. Soften the yeast in the warm water. When the mixture foams, add it to the mixture in the crock. Cover the crock with three layers of plastic netting or cheesecloth, and place the cover loosely over the crock. Store the crock at room temperature (70 to 75° F.) and stir the mixture daily.

On the fifth day, strain the mixture through a few thicknesses of plastic netting or cheesecloth. Wash the crock thoroughly, and return the mixture to it for a second stage. Add the vinegar, which may be from a previous batch of malt vinegar or any other vinegar. Add a pint of raw apple juice, which can be made by juicing about 1½ pounds of sound apples in an electric juicer, or commercial sweet unpasteurized apple cider made without preservatives. Cover the crock and store it at room temperature for a few days. The surface will develop a grayish film. Allow this to remain undisturbed on top of the liquid for about a month. The mixture will develop a distinctly acid taste. Carefully remove a sample with a teaspoon and taste it. When the taste has reached the desired strength, skim and strain the liquid, pour it into clean glass bottles and cork them tightly.

This recipe makes about 3½ gallons of vinegar. It can be used immediately, or allowed to ripen further in the bottles. In time, it will mellow and have a distinctive flavor. Save a portion of this batch to use as a starter for a subsequent one.

You can pasteurize the vinegar by placing the bottles of vinegar, lightly corked, in a dishpan or another large vessel filled with cold water. Heat it gradually until the water reaches a temperature between 140 and 145° F. Hold it at this temperature for ½ hour; then allow the bottles to cool. Pasteurized vinegar will not form a "mother," nor does it become cloudy. Pasteurization will improve the keeping qualities of the vinegar, especially if the bottles are only partially filled.

HOMEMADE HERB VINEGAR

Convert any vinegar into an herbed one. Use either fresh or dried herbs. Basil, dill, mint or tarragon are especially good. Place one of the herbs, along with the vinegar, in a clear glass jar. Cover and allow the jar to stand for 2 weeks in a sunny window. Each day shake the jar. When the flavor tastes sufficiently strong, strain out the herb, rebottle and cork.

Along with the herb used, you can steep any of the following for a short period of time: finely chopped fresh chives, celery leaves or garlic. Place any of these ingredients in a square of plastic netting or cheesecloth, gather up the corners, tie them together, and allow enough string so that you can lower the bag into the jar and retrieve it. Steep the bag in the vinegar for 24 hours and then remove it.

HOMEMADE WINE VINEGAR

Keep the unused portion of an opened bottle of dry wine at room temperature, for a few weeks. Leave it uncorked but cover the top of the bottle with several layers of plastic netting or cheesecloth. Gradually the wine will convert to wine vinegar.

HOMEMADE HONEY VINEGAR

5 quarts water
1 quart honey
½ cup vinegar

Boil together the water and honey. Allow the mixture to cool and pour it into a clean crock. Add the vinegar, mix well, cover and store the crock in a warm place. Remove any scum that may form on the top while the mixture ferments. After a few weeks, vinegar will form. Strain, bottle and cork it.

HOMEMADE BEET VINEGAR

Beet vinegar, also called rosel or russell, is a clear bright-red vinegar with a winelike aroma. It is used during the Jewish Passover, and to make a Russian-type beet soup.

1 dozen large beets
cold water

Peel and quarter the beets. Place them in a stone crock and cover them with cold water to within an inch of the top of the crock. Cover the crock with a piece of plastic netting or cheesecloth. Place the crock cover at a slight angle, to allow some air to enter the crock. Allow the mixture to stand at room temperature until it turns to vinegar. This will take 3 to 4 weeks. Skim the surface carefully, strain, bottle and cork.

BASIC DRESSING (IN BLENDER)

2 cups vegetable oil (your favorite)
1 cup vinegar (your favorite)
1 teaspoon herbs and seasonings (your favorites)

Blend until smooth. Makes 3 cups of dressing.

Plan to make several different variations of this basic dressing whenever you prepare it. Try adding some of the following ingredients, and experiment with others: sprigs of parsley; a clove of garlic; pieces of pimento; crumbles of blue cheese; a slice of raw onion, tomato, avocado or papaya. Pour a measured portion of the basic ingredients into the blender; add another special ingredient of your choice. Blend and pour the contents into a refrigerator-storage jar. Then pour another measured portion of the basic ingredients into the blender and add a different special ingredient of your choice. Blend and pour the contents into another refrigerator-storage jar. Repeat this preparation several times. You will have prepared several different dressings quickly and easily, and you will have a choice of dressings for your daily salads. If the container of your blender is interchangeable with a screw-top canning jar, as some blender containers are, you can prepare the salad dressings *directly* in the canning jars.

MOCK MAYONNAISE

This recipe is actually a variation on the basic dressing, but it is thicker and creamier. It is risky to use real mayonnaise—which requires uncooked eggs—due to the prevalence of salmonellosis. The pathogen salmonella is frequently found in raw egg and can cause serious gastrointestinal upsets. This mock mayonnaise, made without raw egg, is a satisfactory substitute for regular mayonnaise.

  1 cup vegetable oil
½ cup vinegar
  1 cup yogurt or sour cream
  1 teaspoon herbs and seasoning

Blend until smooth. Add other ingredients to vary the dressing. Makes 3 cups of thick dressing.

Garnishes for Salads

Use garnishes to give that finishing touch to your salad creation. You will experience what the artist must experience when he adds his signature to the finished work. The following are a few suggestions for garnishing a salad.

—Quarter or slice hard-cooked eggs.
—Sieve hard-cooked egg yolks or chop the whites.
—Peel hard-cooked eggs and submerge them in beet juice. Refrigerate them for 3 days. Then remove the eggs, drain, slice or quarter them. The yolks will remain yellow and the whites will be stained shocking pink.
—Cut circles or thin strips of red and green peppers.
—Slice carrots into thin strips, cubes or circles.
—Slice avocadoes into thin strips or cubes.
—Slice raw onions, especially Bermuda or Spanish onions paper thin and separate them into rings.
—Soak raw onion rings overnight in beet juice. Drain the bright-red rings and arrange them on top of any mixed green salad.
—Add sunflower or pumpkin seeds, toasted soybeans, sprouts, ripe olives or raw, unsweetened coconut shreds.
—If you have a flower garden, grow nasturtiums. Add the colorful blossoms to a mixed green salad. First be sure to check for black aphids, especially under the petals. Use nasturtium leaves, blossoms and fruits (capers) as well as the blossoms.
—Add purple violets to the salad. These springtime blossoms are rich in ascorbic acid.

Be creative with your garnishes, varying color, texture and flavor. Bon appétit!

Suggested Reading

Chamber's Encyclopedia. Philadelphia: J. B. Lippincott, Vol. 10, 1895, "Vinegar," p. 485.

Encyclopaedia Britannica. Chicago: The University of Chicago, Vol. 23, 1948, "Vinegar," pp. 169–70.

Hunter, Beatrice Trum, *Fermented Foods and Beverages, An Old Tradition.* New Canaan: Keats Publishing, 1973, "Vinegar: A By-product," pp. 75–79.

Hunter, Beatrice Trum, *The Natural Foods Primer: Help for the Bewildered Beginner.* New York: Simon and Schuster, 1972.

Loewenfeld, Claire, and Back, Philippa, *Herbs, Health and Cookery.* New York: Hawthorn Books, 1967.

Nutrition Notes. Washington, D.C.: United Fresh Fruit and Vegetable Association (newsletters).

Truax, Carol, *The Art of Salad Making.* New York: Bantam, 1971.

USDA publications:

Food, Yearbook, 1959, pp. 242; 479; 547.

Food Guide for Older Folks, Home & Garden Bulletin No. 17, 1970, p. 11.

Green Vegetables for Good Eating, Home & Garden Bulletin No. 41, May 1959, pp. 14–15.

Storing Perishable Foods in the Home, G78, 1971.

Vegetables in Family Meals, Home & Garden Bulletin No. 105, 1970, pp. 30–31.

Western Ways with Fresh Vegetables and Melons. Western Growers Association, 1968, pp. 38–65.

3 *Sprouts*

⚘

Grow a fresh crop of vegetables in your kitchen every day of the year. Centuries ago the Chinese learned how to do just this by sprouting mung beans. You can sprout these, or any other whole dried bean, seed, pea or grain.

Although you can buy canned bean sprouts, homegrown ones are more flavorsome and crisp. Sprouting is a simple procedure requiring no special equipment. You will enjoy producing, at little effort or cost, a nutritious and versatile food.

Buying Seeds to Sprout

Generally, health-food stores are the most reliable sources for seeds intended for sprouting. Regular grocery stores may carry a few seeds, notably dried whole peas or lentils, but such products are apt to be unsatisfactory. While such peas or lentils are fine for cooking, they will sprout poorly, if at all. Most likely they have been washed, heated, dried, fumigated, shaken, cleaned, broken and/or stored for a long time. Each of these processes will lower their viability.

Never buy seeds intended for planting. Garden or farm seeds, or seeds sold by catalog, may have been treated with poisonous pesticides or dyes. Do not assume that the *absence* of warning or process information means that it is safe to use seeds for sprouting. For example, alfalfa seeds and red clover seeds of foreign origin, including those from Canada, are required by law to be stained with methyl violet, methyl red or methyl orange, but there is *no* label warning that such seeds contain these harmful dyes or that the seeds are not intended for human consumption. Some packaged sunflower, millet and other birdseed species may display a warning, "Not for human food," without amplification. It is *likely* that chemicals, legal for seed treatment but illegal for food use, have been applied. Also, I do not advise you to buy seeds for sprouting from farm seed dealers, although some may be safe—for example, grain dealers who sell feed for poultry and cows may sell chemically free seeds since their feed must be approved for pesticide residue levels. Cow feeds, especially, must be chemically safe.

Although sprouting seeds from health-food stores will, of necessity, be more expensive than those from seed dealers, because of the size of the package and the care taken to have them free of pesticide, the cost per serving is still nominal. The safety feature makes this choice of paramount importance.

In nature, all seeds sprout. But not all seeds make good sprouts to eat. Nuts, such as butternut or hickory, would be nearly impossible because of their hardness and size. Poisonous species, such as castor bean, apple, stone fruits, poison ivy, sorghum, sudan grass, potato and tomato are all poisonous. Nor should you try to sprout any plants used for drug purposes. Species that have hard seeds, such as birdsfoot trefoil, will only sprout partially, and many will be wasted.

Which seeds *are* desirable for sprouting as food? Many will be found in health-food stores, and others can be harvested from plants gone to seed in a garden, if you have one.

Legume seeds: alfalfa, chick pea, clover, cranberry pea, fava bean, field pea, kidney bean, lentil, lima bean, marrow bean, mung bean, peanut, pinto bean, soybean

Grain seeds: barley, buckwheat, corn, millet, oat, rice, rye, wheat

Vegetable seeds: beet, celery, chard, cress, kale, lettuce, onion, pumpkin, radish, squash, turnip

Herb seeds: caraway, chia, dill, fenugreek, mustard, parsley, radish

Weed seeds: barnyard grass, kale, lamb's quarter, pigweed, purslane

Oil seeds: flax, safflower, sesame, sunflower

Of the above, the seeds for sprouting purposes most commonly found in health-food stores are alfalfa, fenugreek, lentil, mung, soybean and sunflower, as well as whole-wheat berries. For the beginner, mung beans are the easiest to sprout; soybeans the trickiest, since they tend to mold.

Sprouting Containers

Although commercial sprouters are sold, they are unnecessary. Many types of containers, readily available at home, are suitable for sprouting. Choose any sound, new container made of unpocked stainless steel, unchipped enamelware, sound glassware or uncrazed crockery. Reject any container made of aluminum or copper, as it may have a toxic effect; and avoid iron containers, which can rust. Whichever container you use, reserve it for sprouting only.

The following are some containers *with natural drainage,* used successfully for sprouting.

Unglazed flowerpot: Soak the pot thoroughly by submerging it in water. Plug the drainage hole with plastic netting, cheesecloth, cork or absorbent cotton. Soak the seeds overnight, drain and place them at the bottom. Cover with a saucer or pot cover and place the flowerpot in a shallow pan of water.

An old-fashioned unglazed butter dish, popular prior to the introduction of electric refrigerators, and still sold in Europe, can also be used—discard the inner glass dish. Treat the unglazed outside dish in the same manner as the flowerpot, except that there is no drainage hole to be plugged.

Unglazed flowerpot saucer: Use two unglazed dish-shaped bases, made to be put under flowerpots. Choose a size from 6 to 12 inches in diameter. Check that they have not been dipped in wax, plastic or other material that would seal the clay. To test, pour a little water into the saucer. If the water soaks through, assume that the saucer is unglazed; if it remains, the saucer has been treated with a sealer. To use the saucers for sprouting, place the bottom dish in a shallow glass pie plate which is slightly larger than the flowerpot saucer. The pie plate will hold enough water to wet the outside of the clay saucer and keep it moist. Use the second saucer as a cover. To clean the cover, merely wipe it with a slightly dampened cloth but do not immerse it in water. To make the cover easy to lift, drill a hole in the center and insert a cupboard knob. This arrangement of flowerpot saucers and pie plate works especially well with small seeds such as alfalfa, clover, radish or mustard.

Colander: Place drained seeds in a colander, set the colander in a large saucepan or bowl and cover it. The colander makes a good sprouter for large seeds, such as corn, lentils, lima beans, peas or soybeans. To use the colander for smaller seeds, line it with two layers of plastic netting or cheesecloth.

Triangular sink strainer: The strainer is designed to hold peelings and other kitchen waste. Place the drained seeds in a new, clean strainer and set the strainer in a large saucepan or bowl. Proceed as with the colander arrangement.

Tea strainer: This is especially good for sprouting small seeds for only one or two servings. Place the drained seeds in the strainer, set the strainer in a teacup or teapot and cover it.

Coffee percolator: Carefully scour a discarded coffee percolator, especially the strainer intended to hold the coffee grounds; or use a new percolator, choosing one made of stainless steel, enamel or porcelain. Place the drained seeds in the strainer, lower the strainer into the pot, and put the cover in place. This container works well with small seeds.

Turkish towel: Soak a Turkish towel in water, wring it out well, place the drained seeds on top, and roll up the towel. Use this arrangement to sprout large seeds, grains or beans.

Sponge: Soak two new synthetic utility sponges in water, wring them out well, and place the drained seeds between the sponges. This arrangement works well with small seeds.

Blotting paper: Soak two new sheets of white blotting paper in water, drain off the excess, and place drained seeds between the sheets. Place the blotting paper on a large, flat tray and keep the blotting paper moist but not soaking wet.

The following are some other arrangements *without natural drainage,* used successfully for sprouting. To compensate for lack of drainage in these containers, it will be necessary to rinse the seeds thoroughly in tepid water several times daily.

Wide-mouthed glass jar: Of all arrangements, I find this to be the simplest and most satisfactory. Choose any ordinary pint-size, quart-size or 2-quart glass jar, depending on the volume of sprouts you wish to prepare. You will be able to do the entire sprouting procedure in the jar: soaking, draining and sprouting. After putting the seeds into the jar for the initial step of soaking, cover the mouth of the jar with two layers of plastic netting or cheesecloth, held in place with rubber bands or strings.

Saucepan, crockery bowl, or glazed, covered casserole: Place the drained seeds in any of these containers and cover with a loose-fitting pot cover or plate. If the casserole has its own cover, place it on top at a slight angle so that some air can enter. If necessary, wedge a toothpick between the casserole and its cover.

Method of Sprouting

Select clean, whole seeds, grains or beans. Remove any debris or broken seeds. Soak one or two tablespoons of seeds in tap water. Remember that the seeds will swell to twice their original size after they are soaked, and they will increase in volume six to eightfold after they have sprouted. Beginners are apt to use too many seeds and to pile them on top of one another. Such crowding cuts off air, which is needed for proper sprouting and should be permitted to circulate around the seeds. Allow the seeds to soak overnight. Then drain off the water, rinse in lukewarm water, drain again, and transfer the soaked seeds to your chosen sprouting container.

From now, the sprouts require only moisture, warmth and darkness. A kitchen cupboard is a satisfactory storage place. If the seeds appear to be drying out, rinse them but don't allow them to stand in water. If you do, they will mold.

Day by day you will be able to watch the miracle of germination and growth. You should be able to observe tiny sprouts beginning to appear within 24 hours after you have put the container in the cupboard. By the end of the second or third day, the sprouts will have roots about a half inch long. The seed coats will still cover most of the cotyledons—the first leaf or pair of leaves developed by the embryo in seed plants.

Sprouts are usually ready to use in three to six days after germination, depending on the seed variety and temperature. You will find that sprouting develops faster in summer than in winter. On the last day of sprouting, transfer the container to a sunny place. The cotyledons will turn green rapidly as they develop chlorophyll. The flavor of sprouts is improved if you allow them to develop chlorophyll.

By now, most of the seed coats will come loose. Like popcorn hulls, these seed coats are edible. You can eat them along with the sprouts. But if you prefer to discard them for appearance, turn the sprouts into a bowl, cover with cool water, and shake them gently with your fingers. Many, but not all of the seed coats will float up to the top of the water and you can skim them off. Drain the seeds well. They are ready to be used. Or you can refrigerate them and store them for a few days.

When Sprouts Are Ready to Use

Both the flavor and palatability of different types of sprouts depend on their degree of growth. Eat them at their prime.

Legume seed sprouts: The soybean or pea sprout should be 2 inches; the mung bean, 1 to 3 inches, or even longer; the alfalfa sprout, 1 to 2 with their little green leaves well developed; and the lentil, only 1.

Grain sprouts: The sprouts of wheat, rye and other grains should be allowed to develop only to the length of the seed. If they are allowed to grow longer, they develop a sweetish but unappealing flavor, and they are excessively chewy. However, if you allow grain sprouts to continue growing so that they develop green leaves, you can snip them off and use them in salad. The leaves are pleasantly sweet. Tiny hair rootlets develop on grain sprouts. These are feeder roots, not mold.

Herb seed sprouts: The fenugreek sprout should be 1 inch.

Oil seed sprouts: The sunflower sprout should be only about ¼ inch long. If you allow it to grow longer, it develops an unpleasant bitterness.

By following these guidelines, you can eat the sprouts at their highest level of nutritional development. With the current effort to stretch the food dollar as far as it will go, and to obtain at the same time the best possible nutritional values, the use of sprouts deserves consideration. Sprouting is an old idea with a new twist to fit modern living. Sprouts, once considered a "health food" or a tasty treat for livestock, have gradually become respectable table fare for all who enjoy good food.

Sprouts: Nutritious and Digestible

Based on information supplied by various researchers, there are few foods more nourishing than seeds, which provide an almost complete life-support system. Seeds are sources of protein, carbohydrate, oils, vitamins, minerals and hormones—all the necessities for the first few days of life of the plant embryo until both sun and chlorophyll can take over the function of food manufacture on a permanent basis. When the seeds begin to germinate, they convert starch into sugar, and their hormone and vitamin content increases. The extent of this increase is phenomenal. The science of sprouting for human food is still relatively new, and data still incomplete. What exists, to date, should convince you that sprouts can make a valuable contribution to the diet.

Workers at the Kansas Agricultural Experiment Station found that in sprouting oats for seven days, the amount of ascorbic acid developed was equivalent to that present in a similar quantity of lime or grapefruit juice. On the ninth and tenth days, the ascorbic acid content had soared to a level comparable to that found in honeydew melon, which is a source even richer than fresh blackberries or blueberries.

At the University of Pennsylvania, it was learned that soybean sprouts increased their ascorbic acid by more than 500 percent within 72 hours.

The sprouting of oats was studied at Yale University. The greatest vitamin increase was found in riboflavin (vitamin B_2). By the fifth day, riboflavin content had increased by 1,350 percent; by the time the tiny green leaves appeared, by 2,000 percent. Sprouted oats also increased in other fractions of vitamin B: thiamine (B_1), 10 percent; pyridoxine (B_6), 500 percent; nicotinic acid, 500 percent; biotin, 50 percent; pantothenic acid, 200 percent; folic acid, 600 percent; and inositol, 100 percent.

Work at the University of Minnesota demonstrated similar vitamin B increases with sprouted wheat.

Sprouts from legumes are higher in protein, amino acids, vitamins and minerals than other sprouts. Alfalfa sprouts are especially high in minerals.

Dr. Francis Pottenger, Jr., a nutritional researcher, found that the protein in sprouts was of high biological quality. Using animals, Dr. Pottenger found that sprouted legumes and grains were able to sustain life through the reproductive cycle for several generations.

Although beans and legumes should not be eaten raw because

they contain certain naturally occurring toxicants, when they are sprouted they lose these undesirable properties. Also, people who find cooked beans and legumes gas-producing and difficult to digest, discover that they can eat sprouts without suffering from such unpleasant digestive disturbances.

Storing Sprouts

Store sprouts as you would store lettuce or celery. Protect the sprouts against moisture loss by wrapping them in a moist towel or salad bag, and place them in the vegetable crisper of the refrigerator. If they age too long, sprouts tend to become bitter because their supply of sugar is eventually exhausted. If you expose them to sunlight during part of each day you store them, you can offset this change somewhat and preserve their green color. Rinse them in cool water daily to prevent them from drying out. Use stored sprouts within a week. If they begin to turn brown, they are past their peak of quality.

Taste Characteristics of Sprouts

Each type of sprout has a different characteristic taste. Experiment to find out which ones appeal to you. Mustard seeds give off the odor of hydrogen sulfide (rotten eggs) when you soak and sprout them. Most of the stronger-tasting species, such as radish, dill, onion and turnip, are high in sulfur-containing amino acids. However, they have a tangy taste and give zip to a salad if you use them occasionally.

Legumes, too, are fairly high in sulfur. Legume sprouts do not taste sweet; lentils, for example, may even be slightly bitter. But many individuals enjoy them in a tossed salad.

By contrast, grains, because of the starchiness of their seeds, produce quite a bit of sugar. (Because of this, grains are used for malting, a process in which starch is converted to sugar and then to alcohol.) The result is that sprouted grains develop a somewhat unappealing sweet flavor if they are eaten alone, or in any quantity. Use them sparingly, shortly after they have begun to sprout.

Using Sprouts

As soon as the sprouts are ready to use, eat them either by themselves or in combination with other foods. Eat them raw, in any type of salad, or even make a salad exclusively of the sprouts, mixed with your favorite dressing. These are a few suggestions. Try your own combinations.

—mixed greens and lentil sprouts
—celery, onion, pimento and mung bean sprouts
—green pepper, carrot and soybean sprouts
—cole slaw and sunflower seed sprouts
—chicken salad and fenugreek sprouts
—fish salad and wheat sprouts
—fruit salad and alfalfa sprouts

Use sprouts instead of lettuce for sandwiches, or blend sprouts into the sandwich spread. Use them as garnishes for soups, casseroles or stews, and as an ingredient in relish.

RAW SPROUT RELISH

1½ cups bean sprouts
1½ cups raw beets, grated
½ cup celery, diced
1 cup fresh pineapple, diced
½ cup pineapple juice, unsweetened

Mix all ingredients together. Serve as a relish with meat, fowl or fish. Makes 5 cups of relish.

If you add sprouts to cooked foods, use them in meat or fish loaf; in scrambled eggs or omelets; in bread dough or muffin batter; or with stewed tomatoes.

Sprouts are used in many exotic Oriental recipes. Adapt them by using familiar ingredients.

SPROUTS ORIENTAL

3 tablespoons vegetable oil
1 cup of any of the following, singly or mixed: sliced mushrooms, onions, scallions, green pepper, celery
seasoning: ginger, garlic, curry, tamari (a fermented soybean sauce) or miso (a fermented soybean paste)
2 cups fenugreek sprouts (or any other large, crisp sprout)

Heat the oil and sauté the mixed ingredients and seasonings briefly. Add the sprouts. Cover the pan and steam over low heat for 3 minutes. Serve over a bed of brown rice. Serves 6.

Use any type of sprout in soup; tangy-tasting sprouts with meats; legume sprouts with vegetables; and grain sprouts with yeast breads. Try the legume sprouts or oil-seed sprouts, such as sunflower, safflower or sesame, with yeast breads.

Legume sprouts, such as mung or soybean, have a somewhat "beany" taste when they are raw. You can make them more palatable by cooking them briefly.

LEGUME SPROUT PATTIES

2 cups mung bean, lentil or soybean sprouts
1 onion, chopped
2 stalks celery, diced
2 eggs, beaten
½ teaspoon each, savory and sage
2 teaspoons tomato juice
1 tablespoon millet meal or cornmeal
   seasoning

Grind the sprouts in an electric blender or in a meat grinder. Blend them with the remaining ingredients and shape the mixture into patties. Sauté them in an oiled skillet until brown on both sides. Serves 6.

Even elderly persons who have chewing difficulties, or persons on a liquid diet, can enjoy sprouts. Fine, tender sprouts such as alfalfa are eaten easily. All sprouts can be added to fruit or vegetable juices and liquified in an electric blender. Try some of these combinations, and experiment with others.

—celery, onion or parsley sprouts with tomato-based drinks
—bland legume, vegetable or oil-seed sprouts with orange, apple, pineapple, cranberry or grape juice drinks

Sprouts are educational. If there are children in your household, let them nurture the growing sprouts. Children enjoy this activity and like to feel that they are contributing toward the needs of the entire family. Sprouting can lead to a better understanding of the plant world and to an appreciation of the marvel of life. Sprouting is the easiest form of gardening, without the problems of rain, hail, drought, insects or crop failure!

Suggested Reading

Courter, Gay, *The Beansprout Book*. New York: Simon & Schuster, 1973.

Elwood, Catharyn, *Feel Like a Million!* New York: Pocket Books, 1970, pp. 278–295.

Hunter, Beatrice Trum, *The Natural Foods Cookbook*. New York: Simon and Schuster, 1961, "Sprouts," pp. 163–65.

Hurd, Frank J., and Hurd, Rosalie, *Ten Talents*. Allegan, Michigan: Allegan Health Clinic, 1968, pp. 287–95.

Liener, Irvin E., "Toxic Factors in Edible Legumes and Their Elimination." *American Journal of Clinical Nutrition*. Vol. 11, October 1962, p. 289.

Van Dyne, Frances O., *Recipes for Using Soybeans*. Urbana, Illinois: College of Agriculture, University of Illinois, Circular 662, June 1950.

Way, Winston A., *Sprouting Seeds—For Fun and Nutrition*. Burlington, Vermont: University of Vermont, Extension Service, Circular 600-i-73-UVM-TV2, January 1973.

Whyte, Karen C., *The Complete Sprouting Cookbook*. Charlotte, Vermont: Garden Way Publishing Co., 1973.

4 *Whole Grains*

"Pigs are better fed than babies." You have probably heard this comment. It is certainly true in terms of what is done with cereal grains.

Throughout history, every agricultural nation has carefully cultivated grains. Cereal grains belong to a great family of grasses. From the earliest times, land creatures—both man and animal—have lived directly or indirectly from the grains produced by these grasses.

The cereal grains continue to furnish a significant portion of the diet of both man and animals. They account for about a quarter of the total food calories of the human population in the United States; and roughly one third for all livestock and poultry.

When cereal grains are prepared for human food, the bran and the germ are usually removed; the part we eat consists almost entirely of the starchy endosperm. But care is taken to include the valuable nutrients when the cereal grains are prepared for animals. Hence, it becomes literally true that pigs are better fed than babies.

Rice

At times you probably use rice as a potato substitute. Rice is a versatile food; it blends well with cheese, egg, milk, cream, fruit, nuts, honey, meat or seafood. You can use rice to stuff fowl, or add it to soups or stews. Many gourmet dishes call for rice as a main ingredient, whether it is Creole *pilau,* Italian *risotto* or Spanish *arroz con pollo.* Many Oriental and Middle Eastern dishes use rice as a base.

Rice ranks third in our country as a staple food grain. In addition to its use as a grain, it appears in some familiar foods and beverages. Rice flour is used as a thickening agent similar to cornstarch or potato flour. The broken rice kernels, screened out from polished rice, are called "brewer's grits" because they are used in beer brewing.

An average American eats a little more than seven pounds of rice a year. The chances are that most of that rice will be polished and white.

White rice is highly processed, with most of its original nutrients removed for aesthetic appeal and good keeping qualities. "Enriched" white rice means that there has been an attempt to restore some of the lost nutrients. "Converted" white rice means that an effort has been made to keep the nutrients from getting lost. The rice is placed under vacuum and drenched with hot water under steam pressure. This process allegedly drives the vitamins and minerals into the starchy part of the rice grain. After the excess moisture is removed, the rice is milled and polished in the usual way. Converted rice contains approximately 85 percent of the vitamins of brown rice.

A new rice-milling process is being developed, in an attempt to produce white rice with a higher protein content. The process is called deep-milling. The rice is tumbled against a rapidly moving abrasive that grinds away the outer surface. The protein content of rice is highest in the outer portions of the kernel, and decreases toward the center. Deep-milling of rice, by driving the protein to the interior of the grain, permits it to retain up to 20 percent protein, compared to only 6 to 9 percent in the entire kernel after the outer portion is removed.

However, if you are concerned about getting the most nutrition for your food dollar, choose brown rice, with its sweet, nutty flavor. USDA nutritionists state that brown rice is the most nutritious of all the rices. Only its hull is removed in milling. The bran, which remains, contains many nutrients, especially vitamin B and minerals.

THE ART OF COOKING BROWN RICE

If you have tried to cook brown rice and have given up in despair because the product turned out to be a mushy, heavy, sticky mess, do try again. Learn to cook brown rice *properly,* and you will overcome these problems. Follow five cardinal rules.

(1) Do not wash rice (brown or white) before cooking it. This is an unnecessary carryover from former times. Today's packaged rice has already been cleaned. Moreover, washing is nutritionally wasteful. If you wash brown rice before cooking, it can lose as much as 10 percent of its supply of thiamine; white rice will lose as much as 25 percent. This loss shortchanges you needlessly, and could be especially important if you serve rice frequently.

(2) Use the proper amount of liquid for cooking brown rice—not too much, not too little. Fortunately, the nutrients in rice can be retained if the rice is cooked in just the liquid it needs to absorb while it cooks. When you prepare brown rice, or any whole grain, a good rule of thumb is to use twice as much liquid as grain. Many kinds of liquid can be used, including water, meat stock, milk, tomato juice or vegetable juice. This gives you a good opportunity to use the mineral-rich juices in which you have steamed vegetables or stewed fruits.

(3) *Bring the liquid to a rolling boil and trickle the brown rice slowly into it, so that the liquid continues to boil. This procedure may take several minutes but it is well worth it,* since it will ultimately eliminate gumminess. This is what happens: as the grains hit the boiling liquid, the starch in the rice immediately cooks; it does not have time to soak out and thicken the cooking liquid, nor does it have time to bind the particles together. If the starch in the rice is allowed to soak out and thicken the cooking liquid, the rice will become mushy.

(4) After all the brown rice is in the pot, cover it tightly, and cook it over a *low* heat until all the liquid is absorbed. This will require about 45 minutes. If the brown rice has finished cooking before you are ready to serve it, place the pot in a larger one containing hot water, and put this double boiler arrangement over low heat to keep the rice hot.

(5) If you want to conserve the nutrients in cooked brown rice, do not rinse it.

There are more than 7,000 known varieties of rice around the world. Most brown rice is straw-colored, but there are also some that are red, brown, purple, black and variegated. Rice differs in the length of the grain. As a rule, the long-grain rice has a slightly higher protein content, while the short-grain rice cooks faster. When you use rice for a side dish, use the long-grain rice. Its grains are tender and don't get mushy when cooked. If you want to use rice for puddings or hot breads, use the short- and medium-grained rice. These grains are moist and somewhat sticky when cooked.

Glutinous rice, grown in China, is sometimes sold in grocery stores in Chinese neighborhoods of large cities. Glutinous rice contains less starch than ordinary white rice, and it has more dextrose, as well as some maltose. It is sticky, and the Chinese use it mainly in sweet desserts. Try different varieties of rice and discover which ones you like best.

The Latin name for rice is *oryza,* from which many names for rice have developed. If you travel in foreign countries it may be helpful for you to spot rice dishes on the menu: *rijst* in Dutch; *riz,* in French; *reis,* in German; *ris,* in Swedish and Danish; *riso,* in Italian; and *arroz,* in Spanish.

Rice is one of the world's greatest crops—much more important than wheat. It is the staple food of over half the human race, so its value can hardly be exaggerated. Rice was probably first cultivated in southeast Asia long before recorded history. From ancient ceremonials we know that it was being cultivated long before 3,000 B.C. In some ancient languages, the word for rice was the same as the word for food. One Chinese dialect used the same word for both rice culture and agriculture. The renewed popularity of this whole grain, brown rice, links us with the past.

Brown rice is only one of several whole grains long in use in other sections of the world. Fortunately, other varieties are now available to Westerners. It is time we became better acquainted with them.

Unpearled Barley

Probably you are familiar with "pearled" barley in Scotch broth or soup. The bran has been removed from the grain, a process similar to the removal of the outer coating of polished rice. Pearled barley is mainly starch. Nutritionally, pearled barley is inferior to unmilled or unpearled barley.

Barley has a venerable history. The ancient Egyptians believed that it was the first cultivated grain. Its introduction was traced back to their goddess Isis. Barley has been found among the ruins of some of the oldest known structures built by man. Recently, stores of barley were found in the Stone Age lake dwellings located in present-day Switzerland. Barley was well known in Biblical times. Although it was used for breads and barley cakes, for the most part it was not cultivated as a human food. It was used mainly for animals, including horses and dromedaries. However, Pliny tells us that the Roman gladiators were called *Hordearii*, because they ate *horeum* (barley) as food.

Barley is a hardy crop that thrives in extremely cold as well as in very hot climates. It grows successfully in Alaska, Siberia and the Arctic Circle; in India; on the Sahara Desert; and in the Himalaya Mountains. Wild barley still grows as a weed in northern Africa and western Asia, from Morocco to the high, dry plains of Turkestan, east of the Caspian Sea.

Barley is especially popular in North Africa and parts of northern Europe, notably in Siberia, Norway, Sweden and Scotland. Although it was once used principally as livestock food for poultry and for fattening swine, it has also traditionally been the mainstay in the diet for humans in some northern European countries. The grain was simply threshed and left loosely surrounded by the husks. This unpearled barley was highly nutritious.

Unfortunately, most of our barley crop still goes to livestock. Small amounts are hulled and milled into pearled barley for soup. The remainder is germinated as barley malt, an ingredient in fermenting alcohol and alcoholic beverages; or it is used as an ingredient in malted milkshakes, special infant and diet foods, and prepared cereals. A very small amount is sold as "naked" or unpearled barley for human food. Generally you can find unpearled barley only in health-food stores.

Cook unpearled barley in the same manner as brown rice (see pages 81–82). It will cook faster than brown rice. Barley will be done in about half an hour. Use barley as a potato or rice substitute or in soup.

Buckwheat Groats

Doubtless you have enjoyed the taste of buckwheat in the popular buckwheat pancakes, perhaps topped with buckwheat honey. Or you may have eaten buckwheat as "kasha," an ethnic term for buckwheat groats. Although groats usually denotes hulled, cracked grain, this generic term can refer to the hulled but whole kernels of buckwheat.

Strictly speaking, buckwheat is not a member of the grass family and is not a true grain. But buckwheat has all of the characteristics and uses as cereal grain, and we tend to think of it along with wheat, rye, oats, barley, corn and millet. Actually, buckwheat belongs to a large family of plants that includes rhubarb, sorrel, bindweed and more than 800 other species.

Originally buckwheat came from north-central Asia, where it still grows wild. In China and other eastern countries, buckwheat was cultivated as a bread grain. The heart of the seed was also cooked. Buckwheat, introduced into Europe in the Middle Ages, became a staple, as porridge, in Brittany and Russia. In many European areas, the poor often mixed buckwheat with a small amount of more expensive wheat flour to make coarse bread. The Dutch brought buckwheat with them to the New World. As early as 1626, buckwheat fields flourished in what is now part of New York City. From there, buckwheat grew wild, especially in eastern United States and southeastern Canada.

Although the nutritional value of buckwheat has been acknowledged, its use has been mainly for animal feed. The seeds of wild buckwheat are relished by bobwhites and other birds. An account, written more than a century ago, describes some of the benefits of buckwheat. One of its principal uses in Great Britain was "to feed pheasants during the winter, in spots set apart for the preservation of that species of game. . . . Such an abundance of their favorite food will not only prevent pheasants from rambling, but frequently allures others from spots where an equally comfortable provision is not made." The writer noted that all animals are fond of buckwheat and thrive on it. When buckwheat was given to cows, it "caused them to yield an abundance of excellent milk, which makes good butter and cheese." Buckwheat groats, mixed with oats, were fed to horses. The reader was admonished, however, against fattening pigs upon buckwheat groats: "If this food be given to them in great quantity at first, it will occasion the animals to exhibit symptoms of intoxication, so that they run squeaking and tumbling about in a grotesque manner. As they become habituated to the use of the grain, such an effect ceases." In addition to buckwheat as animal feed, "In Brabant [Belgium] it is not unusual for persons who derive a profit from keeping bees to sow this grain near their dwelling, they being of opinion that no plant is equal to it for affording to those insects a proper supply of materials whence their sweet store is elaborated." Today, many beekeepers continue to plant fields of buckwheat. Another old farm practice noted was that "buckwheat is sometimes sown in order that the plants may be ploughed into the ground, and serve as manure in the process of bringing lands into proper order for other crops." Today, many farmers still follow this practice of turning under green crops.

Buckwheat used to be a major crop in the United States, and although its production in America has dropped to only a fraction of what it was a century ago it is still cultivated extensively in Europe. Presently buckwheat ranks only eleventh in our grain harvests. Cultivated buckwheat grows mainly in New York State and in Pennsylvania, and in lesser amounts in West Virginia, Michigan, Ohio and Wisconsin.

You can buy raw or toasted buckwheat groats in health-food stores and in specialty sections of supermarkets. Use it as a potato or rice substitute, as well as a cooked breakfast cereal.

Buckwheat groats are exceedingly soft. This feature lets you cook buckwheat much faster than the true cereal grains. In cooking buckwheat, use my recommended proportions of two parts liquid to one part grain. Bring the liquid to a rolling boil. Trickle in the buckwheat groats. Cover the pot and *turn off the heat.* Allow the groats to absorb all of the liquid. *In five minutes the buckwheat will be ready to eat.*

Since buckwheat is so soft, you can grind a small quantity of uncooked buckwheat groats in an electric blender and make your own buckwheat flour. Use it for buckwheat pancakes and other baked goods, as well as a thickening agent in soups, gravies and dressings.

Both buckwheat groats and flour should be fresh, for their high fat content can in time turn buckwheat rancid. Refrigerate buckwheat products in warm weather.

If buckwheat is consumed in very large quantities, it can cause a rash to appear on the skin of man, and on white-colored animals, especially on animals exposed to direct sunlight. On the other hand, since buckwheat is not a true grain, it is sometimes well tolerated by people who are allergic to cereal grains such as wheat, corn and rye.

Buckwheat is tasty and nutritious. Become better acquainted with this well-known food of yesteryear.

Millet

You have probably seen a panicle of millet hanging in a birdcage. Songbirds, as well as livestock and poultry, are fond of it. At times it has been called "fodder millet" or "hog millet." As for humans, millet is used to feed the world's poor. Millet was called "Guinea corn" in the early West Indian colonies, either because it was introduced from the west coast of Africa or because it had been extensively used to feed African Negroes in the colonies. In Africa, millet was sometimes the principal food and sustained both humans and their domesticated animals. At times the poor simply parched the millet and used it without further preparation. Or they crushed the grains and steeped them in water. Or they husked the grains, pounded and mixed them with melted fat and made an edible paste of it.

Millet has always been recognized as a nutritious food. Indeed, millet, not rice, was the traditional cereal staple for northern China, Africa and India.

Most of the millet grown in the United States is used for birdseed mixtures. People are beginning to realize however, that millet can also make an important contribution to the human diet. You can buy it at health-food stores, or in some specialty sections of supermarkets. Millet seeds vary greatly in size, shape and color. The commonly available ones are tiny, shiny-white or cream-colored ovals.

Use millet as a potato or rice substitute and as a cooked breakfast cereal. To cook it, follow the proportions of two parts of liquid to one part of grain. It will be ready to eat in about half an hour.

Bulgur

If you have ever eaten pilaf in a Near Eastern restaurant you probably ate bulgur, which had been seasoned and cooked in broth or soup stock. Bulgur, sometimes spelled bulghur or bolgur, is cracked, parched wheat that has retained the bran and germ. Long in use in the Near East, bulgur is increasingly popular with those who are trying this versatile food for the first time.

Before bread was baked, people made bulgur from wheat. They roasted the grain in open braziers and spread it out to dry in the sun. They rubbed the parched wheat to remove some of the bran and then cracked the wheat to a coarse or fine meal with a mortar and pestle. After the autumn wheat harvest, it was common practice in the Near East for every household to prepare an entire year's supply of bulgur. People discovered that bulgur stored well and resisted insect infestation.

During the fourteenth century, Armenians who traveled to other lands carried bulgur with them and introduced it to many areas of the world.

Modern American flour mills prepare and ship bulgur to many foreign markets. The old process is somewhat improved by technological advances. WURLD wheat, a new product name for bulgur, reflects both its worldwide use and the whirling action that gently removes the bran. In this new process, developed by USDA, almost all of the niacin, choline and minerals of the original wheat are retained, as well as the whole endosperm, including the nutritious aleurone layer. More than half of the thiamine, riboflavin, pyridoxine, pantothenic and folic acids of the original wheat remain in the new product. WURLD stores as well as ordinary bulgur.

Commercially prepared bulgur is packaged and sold in many supermarkets (sometimes under the name Ala) because of its popularity with some ethnic groups. It is also packaged with prepared seasonings and sold as pilaf. Bulgur is sometimes sold in bulk in health-food stores and in cities, especially where there is a large population of Near Easterners. You can buy finely or coarsely cracked bulgur. The latter has a more nutlike texture.

Mormons are urged to stock at least a year's supply of durable foods in their households, and many of them store wheat. Some prepare their own bulgur from the wheat. You, too, may enjoy preparing your own bulgur.

Homemade Bulgur Processing

Obtain clean wheat berries intended for human consumption. Do not use treated seeds intended for planting. Rinse the wheat in cool water and pour it into a large pot. Cover it with fresh water, then cover the pot and steam the wheat from 35 to 45 minutes or until most of the water is absorbed and the wheat is somewhat tender. (Whole-wheat berries taste somewhat rubbery, regardless of how long they are cooked.) Drain off the excess water and spread the wheat on cooky sheets or in shallow pans. Parch the wheat in an oven set at 200° F. or place it in the sun, leaving it until the berries are dry enough to crack easily. Test them by wetting the surface of the dried wheat berries slightly so that you can rub the kernels between your hands. This will loosen the chaff enough so that you can remove it. Using a hand or electric mill or grinder (see pages 206–10), crack the wheat moderately fine. Put the bulgur in tightly closed containers and store in a cool, dry place.

Cook bulgur as you cook rice. Bulgur is as versatile as rice, but less starchy. Bulgur will cook in about half an hour. Use it as a potato or rice substitute; as a cereal; or as a meat extender. Soak bulgur overnight, add it to yeast doughs, and you will have a nut-like flavor and texture in your breads, rolls and cookies.

Whole Grain Dishes

After you cook basic whole grains, turn them into tempting dishes. Use following recipes and let them suggest even more possibilities. Interchange the various whole grains and create your own combinations. Use different cooking liquids. Add various bits of other foods and flavorings. Serve these foods hot or cold, as side dishes, as main dishes, as extenders, desserts, cereals, or even in salad (as Tabouli—see page 95).

SAVORY RICE

This dish is a good accompaniment to cold meat, fowl or fish.

3 cups brown rice, cooked but unseasoned
1 cup seasoned stock
3 scallions and tops, chopped
1 clove garlic, minced
¼ teaspoon ginger, ground
½ teaspoon each allspice and cinnamon, ground
¼ cup almonds, slivered
¼ cup raisins, soaked and drained

Mix all ingredients together and turn the mixture into the top of a double boiler. Cook gently over hot water until the mixture is thoroughly heated. Serves 6.

BARLEY-MUSHROOM CASSEROLE

This dish goes well with hot roast beef.

3 tablespoons vegetable oil
1 pound mushrooms, sliced
2 onions, sliced
⅛ teaspoon curry powder
1 teaspoon tamari sauce
1 cup water
3 cups unpearled barley, cooked but unseasoned

Sauté mushrooms and onions in oil. Add curry, tamari and water. Cover the pot and allow the mixture to cook for 5 minutes. Remove from the heat, add barley and mix thoroughly. Turn the mixture into an oiled casserole, cover and bake at 300° F. for 20 minutes or until the mixture is thoroughly heated. Serves 6.

BUCKWHEAT CEREAL

This hearty hot cereal is prepared quickly and easily.

2 cups water
1 cup buckwheat groats
¼ cup sunflower seeds, hulled

Bring the water to a rolling boil. Trickle in the buckwheat. Cover the pot and turn off the heat. After 5 minutes all the water should be absorbed by the groats. Add the sunflower seeds, mix and serve, topped with light cream or milk, and sweetened, if desired, with a small amount of honey. Serves 6.

OLD-FASHIONED RAISED BUCKWHEAT PANCAKES

You will have to start the preparation for these pancakes the night before you plan to serve them, since the batter is raised overnight with baking yeast.

Long before the "invention" of nonstick cookware, soapstone griddles were in use. Our colonists had learned from American Indians that the naturally slippery surface of soapstone provided an ideal means of cooking without fat or oil. In recent years it has been difficult to find sources for new soapstone griddles. Vermont quarries are back in operation, and new soapstone griddles are available again (see Appendix).

1 teaspoon baking yeast granules (or ⅓ cake of baking yeast)
¼ cup warm water
1 tablespoon unsulfured molasses
½ teaspoon sea salt
1⅓ cups buckwheat flour
½ cup Cornell Mix (see pages 104–05)
1 pint milk (about)

In the evening, soften the yeast in warm water. Allow it to bubble. Add the rest of the ingredients, using enough milk so that the batter is thin. Pour the batter into a large pitcher with enough empty space at the top so that the batter can rise without overflowing. Cover the pitcher and store at room temperature overnight. The next morning, stir down the batter and pour it onto a hot, unoiled soapstone griddle or into a heated, oiled iron skillet. Brown lightly on both sides. Serve with fruit or cottage cheese. Serves 4 to 6, depending on the appetites.

MILLET SOUFFLÉ

Although whole grains are nourishing, none of them are sources of high-quality protein. Combined with cheese, milk, eggs, meat, poultry or fish—which are reliable sources of high-quality protein—the protein quality of whole grains is markedly improved.

1 cup milk
4 egg yolks, beaten
2 cups millet, cooked in milk
½ cup sharp Cheddar cheese, grated
4 egg whites, beaten stiffly

Combine all the ingredients, except the egg whites, and mix them thoroughly. For a good texture, use the electric blender. Turn into a bowl and fold in the beaten egg whites. Turn the mixture into an oiled casserole and bake uncovered in a pre-heated oven set at 350° F. Do not open the oven door while the soufflé is baking. It should be ready in half an hour. Serve at once. Serves 6.

MILLET DESSERT

This dessert tastes good served either hot or cold. It is like a fancy rice pudding.

2 cups millet, cooked but unseasoned
1 cup milk
3 eggs, beaten
3 tablespoons honey or unsulfured molasses
½ cup raisins or dates cut into small pieces
   nutmeg, grated

Blend the millet, milk, eggs, sweetening and fruit together. Turn the mixture into 6 oiled custard cups. Dust the tops with nutmeg. Bake in a moderate oven (350° F.) for half an hour, or until it is firmly set. Serve hot or cold, with milk or light cream. Serves 6.

TABOULI SALAD

You may not think of using cereal grains for salad, but Tabouli is a traditional Near Eastern salad made with bulgur.

1 cup water, hot
1 cup bulgur, uncooked
⅓ cup vegetable oil
⅓ cup vinegar
3 tomatoes, cut into small pieces
3 tablespoons parsley, minced
1 onion, chopped
1 green pepper, chopped
1 clove garlic, minced

Pour hot water over bulgur in a bowl. Stir and allow the bulgur to soak up the water. Then refrigerate overnight or at least a few hours. Add the remaining ingredients, mix thoroughly and chill. Turn the mixture onto a bed of crisp salad greens. Serves 6.

Grinding Whole Grains

By cracking whole grains, you can make grits, coarse meal or fine flour. Grits are good as cereal, while meals or flours are good for baked goods. You can crack a small amount of whole grain into grits with a mortar and pestle or a rolling pin. You can grind a little whole grain into meal if you have an electric blender. Turn the switch on and off several times. Some of the newer models of electric blenders have a "pulse speed," which does this automatically. You can also use an old-fashioned coffee mill or a newer electric coffee grinder for making meal, regulating the texture.

In order to obtain fine flour, however, a grinding mill is most satisfactory (see Appendix). The more expensive ones are the electric models, but if you cannot afford an electric-powered grinding mill, or lack electricity, you may wish to consider a hand grinder. A great deal of physical strength is required to grind enough flour by hand for bread-making, and the flour is usually not very fine. However, it is not arduous to produce a small amount of cracked grain for cereal by means of a hand grinder. Some hand mills can be electrified. If you are handy, you can adapt one, using a secondhand or new motor.

Enjoy Whole Grains, but Don't Go Overboard

By all means use whole grains such as brown rice, unpearled barley, buckwheat groats, millet and bulgur, in addition to the more familiar wheat, rye, oats and corn. But don't use them to such an extent that you upset the balance of your diet. The inclusion of the "Basic Four" is still a sensible guide for daily food choices. Grains are but a part of the Bread-Cereal group; there remain the Meat Group (meat, poultry, seafood, eggs), the Produce Group (fruits and vegetables) and the Milk Group (milk, cheese, etc.).

Plant proteins from grains, beans, legumes and seeds are incomplete in some respects. Do not consume them in large quantities, to the exclusion or reduction of your use of other foods. The human body needs a certain amount of the trace element zinc in order to make use of protein in any form. All the above mentioned plant-protein sources contain a substance known as phytate. Phytate "locks up" the zinc in the body, making the trace mineral unavailable to the digestive system. This locking-up process occurs in varying degrees. *Unless your diet contains a good supply of zinc, the phytate in plant products may bind up enough zinc to keep your body from making full use of the protein you consume.* Perhaps as much as 80 percent of the American population is marginally deficient in zinc. While a slight deficiency may not produce visible symptoms, when your diet depends mainly on plant proteins you may eventually suffer a severe zinc deficiency. This also holds true if you eat meat or fish only occasionally and rely too heavily, out of habit or for other reasons, on grains, beans, legumes and seed products. The only fairly reliable sources of zinc are animal products, which, while containing little or no phytate in themselves, help to counteract the phytate found in plant protein. Also, when you use grains as bread flours, *use leavening.* Investigators found that the phytate problem was intensified among Iranians, who use large quantities of *unleavened bread.* It is believed that the leavening somehow inactivates the phytate, which otherwise causes mineral losses in those who consume the bread.

So continue to enjoy the whole grains, but don't overdo it.

Suggested Reading

Bulgur Associates, Inc., *Selected Recipes Using Bulgur, A New Wheat Food*. Washington, D.C.: 752 National Press Building (updated).

Fenton, Carroll Lane, and Kitchen, Herminie B., *Plants That Feed Us, the Story of Grains and Vegetables*. New York: John Day, 1956.

Gray, Eden, and Cohen, Mary Beckwith, *The Harvest Home Natural Grains Cookbook*. Brattleboro, Vermont: The Stephen Greene Press, 1972.

Hunter, Beatrice Trum, *The Natural Foods Cookbook*. New York: Simon and Schuster, 1961, "Grains," pp. 150–162.

Hylander, Clarence J., *The World of Plants*. New York: Macmillan, 1947, "The Grasses and Cereals," pp. 503–518.

Oberleas, D., Muhrer, M. E., and O'Dell, B. L., "The Availability of Zinc from Foodstuffs." Prasad, Ananda S., *Zinc Metabolism*. Springfield, Illinois: Charles C Thomas, 1966, pp. 225–238.

Rhind, William, *A History of the Vegetable Kingdom*. London: Blackie & Son, 1855.

Rosenvall, V., Miller, M., and Flack, D., *Wheat For Man, Why and How*. Salt Lake City: Bookcraft, 1966.

Standard, Stella, *Whole Grain Cookery*. New York: Paperback Library, 1972.

USDA publications:
  Conserving the Nutritive Values in Foods, Home & Garden Bulletin, August 1965, pp. 13–14.
  "Deep Milling of Rice." *Agricultural Research*, November 1964, p. 11.
  Grasses, Yearbook, 1948.
  Seeds, Yearbook, 1961.
  "WURLD Wheat Has More Vitamins." *Agricultural Research*, February 1965, p. 15.

5 The Cornell Mix

🌱

If you would like to improve the nutritional quality of your baked goods, try the Cornell Mix. The special features of this mix are the use of *unbleached* flour and the additions of soybean flour, milk powder and wheat germ.

History of the Cornell Formula

The Cornell formula was created over thirty years ago by Dr. Clive M. McCay, Professor of Animal Nutrition at Cornell University. His was a pioneer effort to improve human nutrition. Today, attempts along similar lines are in progress.

Dr. McCay had been conducting a series of experiments to study the effects of nutrition on the life span of fish, white rats and dogs. By giving these animals ample amounts of proteins, minerals and vitamins in their diets, but at the same time curtailing their total caloric intake, Dr. McCay was able to slow down both the animals' growth rate and the onset of senility. In some cases the treated group lived twice as long as the control group. The implications seemed clear: if the animals were well fed but not overfed, they could enjoy good health and long life. Could this be applied to humans? Dr. McCay thought it possible. "The nutritional status of every person," wrote Dr. McCay, "lies largely in his own hands during the latter half of life and depends largely upon his ability to curb his intake of such common foods as sugar, alcohol, low-grade cereals and many fats, as well as his ability to select foods of high nutritional value."

At the time of Dr. McCay's experiments, he was asked for suggestions to help improve the diet of patients in mental hospitals in New York State. Dr. McCay chose bread as the staple which could offer the best possibility for improvements. At the time, bread constituted a large portion of the total diet for many people, and especially those who had suffered from the Depression of the 1930's. Numerous surveys revealed grave nutritional deficiencies. Official United States records of those years show that white-flour products constituted about 55 percent of the total food intake of the average city dweller. Patients at mental hospitals were eating even more bread than the general public. Nutritionists commonly acknowledged that the commercial white breads being consumed at that time lacked many essential constituents which had been removed or destroyed in grain-milling and processing. Dr. McCay believed that improved bread could be the most beneficial single nutritional factor, not only for mental patients, but for the entire population.

Dr. McCay's task was to develop a bread that *would be as acceptable* as ordinary white bread in its appearance and taste. At the same time, the ingredients had to be easily accessible to the baker, the dough had to handle easily and the cost of the loaf had to be competitive with the ordinary one. This was a challenging assignment, and it resulted in Dr. McCay's development of the Cornell formula.

Bread made with the Cornell formula was not only accepted

by the mental hospitals, but the formula was offered to anyone who was interested. Bread made from the Cornell formula was served in some school lunch programs; it was made by some commercial bakeries, notably small specialty ones and co-op members; it was demonstrated by some extension service personnel; and it was used by home bakers. The recipe was included in many standard cookbooks, including *The Fanny Farmer Cookbook.*

The Cornell Formula Versus Enriched Bread

The idea of an improved bread continued to grow, but efforts were stymied by the large commercial bakers. They viewed the Cornell bread as a threat. They had already committed themselves to "enrichment" of their products.

The idea of "enrichment" came about when scientists were learning how to synthesize vitamins. Three fractions from the vitamin B complex (thiamine, riboflavin and niacin) had already been synthesized. The Council on Food and Nutrition (then known as the Committee on Foods) of the American Medical Association (AMA) first suggested in 1936 that these three vitamins should be added to white flour. Two years later, the same Council met jointly with the Council on Pharmacy and Chemistry of the AMA, and the principle of food enrichment was endorsed. On March 18, 1939, the Council on Food and Nutrition adopted a resolution encouraging the "restorative" addition of vitamins, minerals and other necessary nutrients to commonly available low-cost foods, including bread and other baked products.

The word "enriched" was used by the Food and Drug Administration (FDA) in May 1940 to describe the addition of thiamine, niacin and riboflavin, as well as one mineral, iron, to flour and bread. The agency established maximum and minimum standards. Calcium and vitamin D were listed as potential ingredients, to be added within specific ranges.

The enrichment program did not attempt to restore all of the vitamins and minerals in whole wheat. It was designed to provide specific nutrients shown to be inadvertently supplied in the diet of many individuals. Flour and breads were chosen as carriers because they were popular, inexpensive and universally available.

Among the many factors *not* restored by the enrichment program are some acknowledged to be vital in human health: vitamins (biotin, pyridoxine and pantothenic acid); minerals (phosphorus, potassium, manganese and copper); and protein amino acids (lysine and tryptophane). These elements, as well as others present in the grain, form an interlocking nutritional mechanism that can be destroyed by the removal or impairment of any one essential factor. For example, even though iron is restored in enriched flour, the copper, needed by the body in order to utilize iron, is not restored. Thus, even after several decades of iron restoration in the enrichment program, iron-deficiency anemia is purportedly widespread. And although calcium is restored in enriched flour, Government surveys show continued calcium deficiency among segments of the population. Doubts about the validity of the enrichment program continue to grow. Despite its shortcomings, however, it should be viewed as an attempt—however limited and futile—to improve the nutritional qualities of white flour and the products made with it.

The Cornell Formula Is Too Good

Protracted hearings were called in Washington, D.C., to establish Federal standards of identity for bread. The hearings began in 1941 and lasted until 1951. Dr. McCay attended the hearings and, in reporting about them in 1952, recalled, "How shall the consumer know what the people in Washington are doing? . . . How many people west of Ohio, or west of the Atlantic seaboard even, ever knew there were any bread hearings unless they were in the technology field? How many consumers were there? Well, very very few. . . . I was a forlorn consumer there. And what did I advocate? I advocated keeping chemicals out of bread until we knew what they really do to the body. I advocated that we honestly tell every consumer on every bread wrapper what he gets in a loaf of bread."

Dr. McCay continued, relating how the baking interests did not wish to state what was in the bread, and how they attempted to keep the Cornell formula out of the bread standards. "How can you buy bread on the basis of value when you do not know what is in that bread? Well, that's the reason in 1942 we became much interested in bread in Ithaca [location of Cornell University]. We had our first open-formula bread there—the bread which we later made in our little co-op store, the triple-rich bread. We developed a bread formula after we weighed very carefully what would taste good. There is no use in developing a foodstuff that does not meet taste appeal. Then we wanted the bread with the highest possible nutritive value at the lowest possible cost. That is the bread that has led to so much controversy and so much bitter attack. We never attempted to put any restrictions on that bread. We never had a penny of money for developing that bread—not a penny of money from the baker, from the miller, from any supplier of any bread ingredient. We have furnished always all the information we had and we have advocated only one thing: that every baker who bakes a bread should put the formula on the label. . . ."

The baking interests succeeded in having the FDA *exclude* the Cornell formula bread from the standards for white breads.

A consumer magazine commented: "The McCay formula bread is clearly superior nutritionally to ordinary bread, and to the extent that the ruling discourages bakers from producing it and consumers from buying it, consumers will be the losers."

Dr. McCay, as the sole consumer voice at the bread hearings, also lost on another issue. The baking interests succeeded in having the FDA exclude ingredient labeling on standardized bread. Even today, consumers continue to suffer from this. It is not mandatory for bakers to list ingredients on the labels of any standardized bread shipped interstate.

The stormy issue of the Cornell formula continued long after the bread hearings ended. The baking interests brought legal suit to prevent the formula from being used. The courts decided that the Cornell bread could be sold, provided that all of the ingredients were plainly printed on the label! How ironic this decision is! The ingredients *not* printed on labels of standardized bread may consist of some 80 ingredients permitted under the Federal Standards of Identity; some have dubious safety records, while others are purely economic shortcuts for the bakers.

THE CORNELL MIX

To make the Cornell Mix, if a recipe calls for 6 cups of flour, measure 6 cups of unbleached white flour into a sifter and add 3 tablespoons of wheat germ, ½ cup of full-fat soybean flour and ¾ cup of milk powder. Blend all of these ingredients together. Sometimes this mixture is called "triple rich" or "high-protein flour" because all three of the additions—wheat germ, soybean flour and milk powder—are protein-rich.

You can use the Cornell Mix with any of your favorite recipes for yeast breads, rolls or cakes; or with quick bread batter for muffins, pancakes or waffles; or with cooky dough. Substitute 1 cup of Cornell Mix for 1 cup of regular flour. You can blend a quantity of the Cornell Mix ahead of time. Store it in the freezer to keep the wheat germ fresh. The mixture is free-flowing as soon as it is taken out of the freezer, but allow it to warm up to room temperature for baking. In general, have all ingredients at room temperature for baking.

If you prefer to prepare the Cornell Mix every time you bake, store the wheat germ in the freezer, once you have opened the container. Keep both the soybean flour and the dry milk powder in tightly closed containers, stored in a cool, dry place.

Dough made with the Cornell Mix handles the same as ordinary dough. After being kneaded, it will be smooth and elastic. The soybean flour gives a golden color as well as a good flavor to baked goods. Use a slightly lower oven temperature, since soybean flour tends to brown baked goods quickly. For example, if you generally bake bread in an oven at 350° F., lower it to 325° F.

About Yeast

Two types of baking yeast are available: dry yeast granules and the traditional compressed cakes of moist yeast. The dry yeast granules have been developed to prolong the active freshness of baking yeast, and this yeast will remain fresh, unrefrigerated, for at least six months. It can be combined with liquids as hot as 110 to 115° F. in a conventional preparation method. When blended with part of the flour—a new mixer method for yeast doughs—liquids as high in temperature as 120 to 130° F. can be used. The advantages of using the dry yeast granules are their long shelf life and their ability to combine with dry ingredients, thus providing added assurance against failures, while eliminating the traditional dissolving step.

Compressed cakes of yeast are the type homemakers have been using for years. The cakes are perishable and must be refrigerated. It is best to use them within a few days after purchase, although they can be frozen wrapped in aluminum foil for up to six months at 0° F. Defrost overnight in the refrigerator before use. Defrosted yeast loses its brittle texture—it will be soft. Compressed cakes of yeast, either fresh or defrosted, should first be dissolved in lukewarm liquid (80 to 90° F.) before they are added to other ingredients.

[If you bake frequently, it is far more economical to buy dry yeast granules in bulk form and avoid expensive packaging. One pound of dry yeast granules equals approximately 48 compressed yeast cakes. Many health-food stores stock El Molino Dry Yeast Granules (see Appendix). Premeasured and dated aluminum-foil-wrapped packets of Fleischman's Yeast, containing the preservative butylated hydroxyanisole (BHA), are commonly sold in supermarkets. Some supermarkets also stock Fleischman's Active Dry Yeast for Bakers in two-pound cans, without BHA (see Appendix). If you use this yeast, be certain to read the directions, since this yeast, intended for bakers, is more concentrated than ordinary yeast (see Appendix). Red Star baking yeasts are also sold in supermarkets. The dry granules are packed in quarter-ounce special envelopes as "Instant Blend Dry Yeast," and the foil-wrapped cakes of compressed yeast, most commonly available, are in ⅝-ounce packets. One- and two-ounce packets are available in some markets.]

This is my adaptation of the Cornell formula, slightly modified, for bread.

CORNELL FORMULA BREAD

Measure 3 cups of warm water (85° F.) into a large bowl. Add 2 tablespoons of dry yeast granules (or 2 packets of compressed yeast, or 2 squares of yeast) and 2 tablespoons of honey. Stir and allow the mixture to stand for 5 minutes.

When the yeast mixture is frothy, stir 1 tablespoon of sea salt, earth salt, or kelp, or a mixture of any of these three seasonings, into it. Add 3 cups of the Cornell Mix, described above. Beat the mixture vigorously, using about 75 strokes if by hand, or beat it for 2 minutes in an electric mixer.

Add 2 tablespoons of vegetable oil, and 3 cups more of the Cornell Mix. Blend all the ingredients thoroughly and turn the dough out onto a floured board. Have additional Cornell Mix handy, since more may be needed. Knead the dough vigorously for about 5 minutes, until it is smooth and elastic. Shape it into a ball, oil it lightly, and place it in an oiled bowl. Cover the bowl and keep it in a warm place (80 to 85° F.) for about 45 minutes, until the dough is nearly double in bulk.

Punch down the dough, fold over the edges, and turn it up-side down in the bowl. Allow it to rise again for 20 minutes.

Turn the dough onto the board, and divide it into 3 equal portions. Fold each one inward and form smooth, tight balls. Cover them with a clean cloth and allow them to rest for 10 minutes. Then shape the balls into 3 loaves, or 2 loaves and a pan of rolls. Place them in buttered bread pans (3½″ x 7½″). Allow the dough to rise in the pans for 45 minutes, or until it has doubled in bulk.

Bake loaves in a preheated moderate oven (350° F.) for approximately 15 minutes; when the loaves begin to turn brown, reduce the temperature (325° F.) and bake 30 to 35 minutes longer.

Remove the finished loaves or rolls from the pans and cool them on racks. If you wish, brush the tops with melted butter. Makes 3 medium-sized loaves.

You can also use the Cornell Mix with whole-grain breads. This recipe calls for whole-wheat flour. Vary it, by mixing in flour made from other grains.

WHOLE WHEAT BREAD WITH CORNELL MIX

Measure 2 cups of warm water (85° F.) into a large bowl. Add 2 tablespoons of dry yeast granules (or 2 packets of yeast or 2 squares of yeast) and ¼ cup each of dark, unsulfured molasses and honey. Stir and allow the mixture to stand for 5 minutes.

When the yeast mixture is frothy, add a beaten egg and 5 cups of finely ground whole-wheat flour. Beat the mixture vigorously, using about 100 strokes by hand, or beat it for 3 minutes in an electric mixer.

Allow the mixture to rest while you measure and sift together in a large bowl an additional cup of whole-wheat flour, ¾ cup of milk powder, ½ cup of full-fat soybean flour, 3 tablespoons of wheat germ, 2 tablespoons of nonleavening brewer's yeast and 2 teaspoons of sea salt, earth salt, or kelp, or a mixture of any of these seasonings.

Work the dry mixture into the yeast mixture until they are thoroughly blended. Knead vigorously and proceed as with the unbleached white flour Cornell Formula Bread given above. Bake at 325° F. for about 1 hour. Remove the breads from the pans and allow them to cool before storing them. For variety, add nuts, raisins or other dried fruit to the dough after you mix the dry ingredients with the yeast mixture. This bread stores well when frozen. Makes 2 large loaves.

Special Features of the Cornell Mix

Milk powder supplies protein as well as liberal amounts of calcium and riboflavin. Two major processes exist for drying milk.

One, spray drying, is relatively harmless to the nutritional value, and apparently does not destroy the important amino acid lysine. The other process, drum or roller drying, however, *is* destructive. The high heat denatures the milk's protein, reduces vitamin C and all other vitamins, and drastically impairs or completely destroys lysine. Unfortunately, processors of milk powder do not specify whether their products have been processed by spray drying or drum drying. Consumers should insist that such information be printed on the milk powder label.

Soybean flour, which is a rich protein concentrate, supplies certain amino acids lacking in wheat flour. Thus it complements the protein of the wheat. The full-fat soybean flour is preferable to the defatted kind because it gives a better appearance and eating quality to the baked goods. However, if you can only find low-fat soybean flour, don't hesitate to use it for making Cornell Formula Bread. (For characteristics of soybean flours, see pages 164–66.)

Wheat germ is a constituent long recognized as rich in many nutrients, especially vitamins B and E, as well as the mineral iron.

Always use unbleached rather than bleached flour. Look for the word "unbleached" on the label. Unbleached flour looks, feels, tastes and handles no differently than bleached flour. The bleaching of flour has been called "social custom and biological stupidity."

The Cornell formula, with its 8 percent milk powder, 6 percent soybean flour and 2 percent wheat germ, added to unbleached flour and other bread ingredients, so improved ordinary bread that animals in Dr. McCay's laboratory were sustained in good health when this bread was used as the sole article of diet. Experiments, repeated at Cornell University, at the School of Medicine at the University of Rochester, by Dr. Estelle Hawley, and at other nutrition laboratories, all confirmed Dr. McCay's findings. White rats fed on bread made with the Cornell formula were able to grow and reproduce even through succeeding generations. By contrast, control rats, fed ordinary white bread, failed to grow normally or to thrive. Their fur became thin, their tails and paws grew scaly and sore, and the animals died prematurely.

History Repeats Itself

Although the development of the Cornell formula by Dr. Mc-Cay made a real contribution to nutrition, it has been largely ignored. Recently there have been new attempts to point out the inadequacies of most commercial white bread and to improve this staple. For example, in 1966, a "special formula" bread containing nutrients not found in enriched white bread was developed and tested on animals by a New York research team. The idea for the new product was prompted by the fact that dietary problems still exist among certain groups of Americans, according to Dr. R. H. Cotton of a large commercial baking company. Dr. Cotton and his associates suggested that the improved bread might benefit the "nutritional status of the individuals in the problem groups," whose nutritional problems tend to persist in spite of the widespread availability of a varied and abundant food supply. Included in these problem groups were teen-agers, the aged, people on diet kicks and those with peculiar dietary patterns.

Although the special-formula bread had not been tested on humans, rat studies suggested that "a similar approach to dietary improvement could be of real significance in human feeding." One group of animals received a special bread containing a larger quantity of milk powder, whole-wheat flour, lactalbumin, egg yolk, and both vitamin and mineral supplements. A control group was fed a commercial white bread. Although, in addition, both groups received similar amounts of other foods found in the typical American diet, the animals fed on the special-formula loaf showed a marked improvement in both weight gain and food efficiency. The special-formula bread increased their growth rate by a minimum of 30 percent. The researchers concluded that "the effects of this change in the nutritional quality of bread, which is well within the limits of technical and economic feasibility for commercial bread production, are especially note-worthy when one considers that bread comprises . . . 22 per-cent of total calories in the diet." The study demonstrated that the special-formula bread diet provided 60 percent more com-plete protein than the standard bread diet. They concluded: "The relative increase in complete protein-calorie ratio, amount-ing to 16 percent, represents a substantial gain in the quality of the mixed diet merely by making a relatively simple adjustment in the quality of the bread used."

On October 21, 1970, Dr. Roger J. Williams, a noted nutri-tional researcher from the Clayton Foundation Biochemical In-stitute at the University of Texas, shocked the country by his findings presented to the National Academy of Science. Dr. Wil-liams reported that two out of three rats, restricted to a diet of commercial "enriched" bread, died of malnutrition within 90 days, and the survivors' growth was badly stunted.

In Dr. Williams' second test, almost without exception, 64 rats managed to survive and grow on a diet of the same bread to which he had added minerals and vitamins, including lysine. He simply replaced the important nutrients removed through milling and processing and added one (lysine) which is lacking in wheat flour. The improved bread was almost indistinguishable from the ordinary one, and the increased cost was nominal.

Dr. Williams charged that "enrichment," as it has been prac-ticed for several decades, is antiquated. "Commercial bread is so deficient it is intolerable in the light of the fact that it can so easily be vastly improved." Dr. Williams contended that "enriched" white bread shows up well in food-composition tables only because it has been enriched with items that are commonly tabulated. Because crucial items that do not appear in the composition tables have been removed, its real value is *lower* than the tables suggest. Dr. Williams blamed the milling and baking interests, as well as FDA, for keeping the enrichment program at a static level. According to Dr. Williams, on the basis of our present knowledge, enriched flour should be called "deficient flour."

Other scientists also are concerned with the same problem. In 1972, two USDA cereal chemists were issued a public patent for making highly nutritious protein-enriched bread. By using up to 16 percent soybean flour or other protein-rich sources, they almost doubled the protein content of ordinary white bread. Currently the protein content of bread is about 8.7 percent; using the soybean flour raises it to about 15 percent. It also triples the concentration of lysine. A spokesman for USDA said, "Such bread can be a principal source of protein, both in developing countries and in the United States, for children and adults whose diets are nutritionally deficient and who depend on bread as a major food."

Since inventions by USDA scientists are made available on a nonroyalty basis, this public patent entitles any baker to use them under "nonexclusive" license arrangements with the department, providing that the facilities and technology meet Federal requirements. It will be interesting to observe whether the baking interests develop this protein-rich bread or allow it to hang in limbo, along with the Cornell formula and Dr. Roger Williams' formula.

If you, as a consumer, cannot find store bread made with the Cornell formula, perhaps you can persuade an enterprising baker in a small shop to make it. The recipe below is also good for school lunch programs, for camps, and for restaurants and communes.

CORNELL BREAD

(Yields 25 loaves)
   8 pounds water, warm
12½ pounds unbleached flour, Northwest or gluten
  12 ounces baking yeast
   4 ounces salt
   4 ounces shortening
   1 pound milk powder
   3 ounces honey
   3 ounces molasses
  12 ounces soybean flour, full-fat
   4 ounces wheat germ

NOTE: Sea salt is preferable to refined salt; vegetable oil is better than hydrogenated shortening; unsulfured molasses is superior to sulfured molasses.

Measure the water into a bowl. Weigh the rest of the ingredients and add them to the water. Mix with a 3-speed mixer at the first speed from 12 to 15 minutes, keeping the dough at 78° to 80° F. The dough should pull away from the bowl; if sticky, add more flour. Cover the dough with a cloth to prevent a hard crust from forming on the top, and keep it between 82° and 85° F. on the dough bench. Allow the mixture to rise 20 to 30 minutes. Divide it into 25 one-pound loaves. Let the loaves rise again about 20 minutes. Then slip them into bread pans and place them in the proofing box, with the temperature between 90° and 94° F., for 20 to 30 minutes, or until the dough has risen to the top of the pans. Bake in a 400° F. oven for 20 to 25 minutes. Remove the loaves from the oven and brush them with shortening.

This recipe is in the public domain, and it can be made without special permission or charge. However, in the spirit of Dr. McCay, who felt strongly that the consumer has a right to know, each baker is requested to print the formula on the wrapper, including the information on the *proportion* in which the ingredients are used. The label on Cornell-formula bread should say that for every 100 parts of unbleached flour there are 8 parts of milk powder, 6 parts of high-fat soybean flour, and 2 parts of wheat germ.

If you are in a position to propose the Cornell formula to large groups, such as hospitals or other institutions, suggest the large-bakery formula below. This is the recipe that was first introduced by the New York State Department of Mental Hygiene in Albany, New York. The original Cornell formula is still being baked in the mental hospitals of New York.

CORNELL BREAD, STRAIGHT DOUGH METHOD

(Yields 200 loaves)
100 pounds unbleached Northwest flour
  72 pounds water, approximately
   2 pounds baking yeast
   2 pounds salt
   4 ounces yeast food
   1 to 2 pounds sugar
   1 pound malt, nondiastatic
   2 pounds shortening
   8 pounds milk powder
   6 pounds soybean flour, full-fat
   2 pounds wheat germ

NOTE: Sea salt is preferable to refined salt; honey or unsulfured molasses is better than sugar; vegetable oil is superior to hydrogenated shortening.

Mixing: Measure the ingredients into the mixer in the order given above. Mix the dough enough to incorporate the ingredients together properly to make a smooth dough. The mixing time will depend on the type and speed of the mixer. Continue mixing until the dough is dry and pliable.

Temperature: The best temperature for rising is between 78° and 80° F. With normal conditions, the dough should be set so that when it is fully matured and ready to be divided, it will be 81° or 82° F. The dough should come out of the mixing machine at a temperature which will give it the proper temperature at the time of its maturity. This means that the dough should be set so that directly after being mixed it will have a temperature of 78° or 79° F.

Fermentation: Allow the mixed dough to rise until it is light. Test it by poking it quickly. The dough should spring back. Turn the dough by pulling the ends and sides well in. Then allow it to rest for half an hour. Turn the dough again, and after 15 minutes take it to the bench or divide it.

Proofing: During the pan proofing, keep the temperature of the proof box between 90° and 94° F., with enough humidity so that the loaves will not form a crust. Be careful not to apply too much moisture to the dough, which contains a high percentage of milk powder. If there is too much moisture, the crust will be undesirably tough and foxy-red in color. To avoid these features, give this dough a little less proofing time before putting it into the oven. If the dough is properly mixed and fermented, it will have a good oven spring.

Baking: If the sugar and malt content are right, both the temperature and time for baking will be the same as for ordinary bread. However, because of the high percentage of milk powder and soybean flour, this type of bread will brown more quickly in the oven than milk- and soybean-free bread. The temperature of the oven should be set so that the loaves begin to color 10 to 12 minutes after they are in the oven. Bake this type of bread at 400° to 440° F. flash heat. Avoid excessive oven temperature at the beginning of the baking or the crust will form too rapidly and the bread will color too deeply. On the other hand, underbaked bread will have an aroma that suggests greenness, and it will be much too moist. When this is the case, it will neither slice nor wrap well.

Suggested Reading

"Bread, A Discussion of What the Food and Drug Administration's New Standards Mean to the Consumer." *Consumer Reports,* July 1952, pp. 343–347.

Cotton, R. H., "Special Formula Bread." *Journal of the American Dietetic Association,* May 1966.

Hunter, Beatrice Trum, *Consumer Beware! Your Food and What's Been Done to It.* New York: Simon and Schuster, 1971, "Our Impoverished Grains," pp. 286–307.

Hunter, Beatrice Trum, *The Natural Foods Primer: Help for the Bewildered Beginner.* New York: Simon and Schuster, 1972, "Cornell Mix Bread," pp. 126–127.

Lear, John, "The Flimsy Staff of Life." *Saturday Review,* October 3, 1970.

McCay, Clive M., and McCay, Jeanette B., *You Can Make Cornell Bread.* Englewood, Florida: Jeanette B. McCay, 39 Lakeview Lane, Englewood, Florida 33533 (pamphlet, $1.25 postpaid).

McCay, Clive M., "The Quest for Better Foods and the Potential Role of Government." *Address,* annual conference, Consumers Union, Kansas State College, Manhattan, Kansas, June 1952.

"New Process Adds Protein to Bread." *New York Times,* October 26, 1972, p. 8.

USDA publications:

"Strengthening the Staff of Life." *Agricultural Research,* November 1968, pp. 8–9.

"Studying the Staff of Life." *Agricultural Research,* July 1972, pp. 10–11.

"The Wheat We Eat." *Agricultural Research,* September 1970, p. 14.

Williams, Roger J., *Nutrition Against Disease.* New York: Pitman Publishing Corporation, 1971, pp. 201–5.

Williams, Roger J., "Should the Science-Based Food Industry Be Expected to Advance?" *Paper,* National Academy of Sciences, Washington, D.C., October 21, 1970.

Williams, Roger J., *et al.,* "The 'Trophic' Value of Foods." *Proceedings* of the National Academy of Sciences. Vol. 70, No. 3, March 1973, pp. 710–13.

6 Sourdough

While enjoying the tantalizing taste and aroma of baked products containing sourdough, you may have wondered what sourdough is and how it is made. If you have eaten sourdough French bread in San Francisco, you have joined many others in considering it one of the major attractions of the city. For over a century, the San Francisco Bay area sourdough French bread has been a celebrated specialty. Many, many attempts have been made to duplicate it elsewhere. But sourdough culture depends on the wild yeasts in the air, and these are very difficult to duplicate.

Wild yeasts, as well as airborne molds and bacteria, are mysterious substances, hard to control. This fact was dramatically illustrated by an incident in cheese-making. A Liederkranz cheese plant was transferred from Eastern United States to the Midwest. The secret formula, the "mother culture" which starts the process, and the equipment were transferred to the new plant. In fact, everything was moved except the shell of the old plant itself. A small contingent of expert Liederkranz cheese-makers began operations in their new headquarters. But the new cheese was distinctly different! No matter how hard the cheese-makers tried, they simply could not duplicate the Eastern plant Liederkranz in the Midwest. Finally, the experts smeared some samples of the original Eastern cheese over the gleaming tile walls of the new plant. After that, the new cheese was satisfactory.

This incident proved to the cheese-makers that the curds are affected by free-floating airborne bacteria as well as by the carefully controlled cultures introduced into them. In the same way, sourdough culture is influenced by the airborne yeasts, and it differs from place to place.

Despite the popularity of sourdough, scientific investigation has only been recently begun to find out what gives it its unique qualities. Researchers are exploring such questions as, What kind of microorganisms are active? What are their functions? Can they be made commercially available? Investigators believe that a process could be developed for adding some sourdough to doughs of other breads to give them some of the taste and appeal of sourdough.

So far, microbiologists have had some surprises. At least two types of microorganisms are responsible for the unique properties of sourdough. Yeasts used for leavening breads cannot tolerate acetic acid; but sourdough bread is highly acetic! At least half of the acid in sourdough bread is acetic acid. The sourdough yeast not only lives in but actually thrives in this acetic medium.

Even stranger, the acid-producing strains of bacteria appear to have a combination of special nutritional and environmental needs for growth, but they do not fit into any presently known scientific classification. For example, they are quite different from the lactic-acid-type bacteria found in sour rye breads.

With the new popularity of both home baking and sourdough, you can buy sourdough starter. (See Appendix.) Or you can make sourdough at home, choosing one of several methods.

HOMEMADE SOURDOUGH STARTER
FROM YEAST DOUGH

Pinch off about a cupful of yeast bread dough just before you are ready to shape the loaves for baking. Roll the dough into a ball. Put it into a clean crock or glass jar—do not use a metal container. The crock or jar should be at least twice as high as the ball because the dough will rise and fall. Cover the crock or jar loosely and let it remain at room temperature. In several days the mixture will have fermented and formed sourdough. It will have a pleasantly sour aroma, somewhat like buttermilk. Add this sourdough to your ingredients when you mix them in the next batch of dough for yeast bread. Again, pinch off a piece of the bread yeast dough just before you are ready to shape the loaves for baking. Take about a cupful and roll the dough into a ball. Wash and dry the crock or glass jar used for the last batch, and put the dough into it. *The dough that is being shaped and baked this time will become sourdough bread.*

HOMEMADE SOURDOUGH STARTER
USING FLOUR

To make sourdough "from scratch" mix 1 cup of warm water with ½ tablespoon of yeast (or ½ cake of yeast) and set it aside for 10 minutes. When it is frothy and active, blend it with 1 cup of flour and an additional ½ cup of warm water. Traditionally, rye flour is used, but any type of flour will do. Pour this mixture into a clean crock or glass jar twice as high as the mixture. Cover it loosely and set it aside for a few days. If bubbles form, you will know that you have successfully captured wild yeasts from the air and that they are thriving in the medium. This sourdough will appear thinner than sourdough made from the yeast bread dough, but it will work as well. Add it to ingredients when you mix them to make a yeast sourdough bread. Again, remember to pinch off a piece of the dough just before you are ready to shape the loaves for baking, and reserve it for subsequent bakings.

HOMEMADE SOURDOUGH STARTER USING ADDITIONS

Another way to make sourdough starter "from scratch" is to gradually add more ingredients to a mixture. Begin by mixing together in a bowl 1 cup of milk or water with 1 cup of whole-grain flour. Cover the bowl loosely and store it at a temperature between 65° and 75° F. Each day, add a small quantity of milk or water with honey (about a tablespoon of liquid and about ½ teaspoon of honey). Stir the mixture after each addition. After about a week, a bubbly mass of sourdough starter should have formed.

HOMEMADE SOURDOUGH STARTER USING POTATOES

Boil 4 pared and cubed potatoes in 1 quart of water. Save the water. When the potatoes are soft, purée and return them to their cooking water. Add ½ cup of honey, 2 teaspoons of salt and 4 cups of flour. You can use the traditional rye flour, but any type of flour will work. Turn the mixture into a clean crock or glass jar and follow the directions given above for making sourdough starter using flour.

HOMEMADE SOURDOUGH STARTER USING HOPS

Simmer 1 cup of hops (see Appendix) with their pollen in 1 quart of water. Cool the mixture and strain out the hops. Return the water to the pot and add 4 medium-size pared and cubed potatoes. Cover the pot and simmer the mixture until the potatoes are soft. Purée the potatoes and add ½ cup of honey. Then add enough flour to make a thick batter. Traditionally, barley flour is used, but any other flour is perfectly acceptable. Soak 2 tablespoons of dried yeast granules (or 2 cakes of yeast) in ¼ cup of lukewarm water. When the yeast is frothy, add it to the batter. Stir well. Turn the mixture into a clean crock or glass jar and follow the directions given above for making sourdough using flour.

HOMEMADE SOURDOUGH STARTER USING MILK

Mix together 1 cup each of milk and flour. Use any type of fluid milk, but skim milk works best. Traditionally, rye flour is used, but any type of flour will work. Turn the mixture into a clean crock or glass jar, cover loosely and allow it to stand at room temperature for 24 hours. Stir in an additional cup of flour. Allow the crock or jar to stand in a warm place for another three days, or until the mixture has a pleasantly sour aroma.

Using Sourdough Starter with Baked Goods

Add any sourdough starter, commercial or homemade, to your favorite recipes for pancakes, waffles, muffins, cookies, cake batters or bread doughs. You can use the sourdough starter as an addition to your usual yeast leavening but baked products that depend solely on sourdough as a leavening agent will not rise as high as they do with other leaveners. Baking soda is often added to sourdough, to boost the leavening action. I avoid the use of vitamin B-destroying baking soda whenever possible, and substitute vitamin B-rich baking yeast instead. If you omit both the baking soda and yeast, the leavening effect of the sourdough will be diminished and the baked goods will not rise very high. Also, the flavor of baked goods will be a little more acid, but completely acceptable. All sourdough products have a pleasant aroma and flavor.

In using sourdough starter, remember that you have added about an additional cup of ingredients to your recipe. If you are an experienced cook who can measure or mix without following a recipe slavishly, you will take this addition in stride by "knowing" just when the batter or dough is right by its appearance or feel. If you are a novice who feels secure in following a recipe to the letter, you may want to figure your ingredient quantities with pencil and paper before you measure them. Whether you work by instinct or calculations, you will discover that when you add sourdough starter you need to *decrease* the amounts of flour and liquid from the original recipe.

Always remember to reserve a cupful of sourdough bread dough or batter for the next baking. Take this out before you shape the dough you are about to bake. If you bake every few days, keep the new supply of sourdough at room temperature in a loosely covered crock or glass jar. If you bake less frequently, slow down the fermentation process by refrigerating the sourdough after it has developed.

Inactivating Sourdough Starter

If you plan not to use sourdough starter for several weeks or longer, freeze or dry it. The Cooperative Extension Service of the

University of Alaska, in describing how sourdough starter can be inactivated before transporting it to camp, made it sound like an animal going into hibernation: "Add enough flour to shape [the sourdough] into a ball, and place it in a sack of flour. In the dried form, the yeast goes into a spore stage that will keep inert for a long time like old-fashioned yeast foam. Water and warmth bring the yeast back to the active stage." You can follow their directions to inactivate sourdough starter in your own kitchen.

Reactivate frozen or dried sourdough when you wish to use it. With care, you should be able to continue the sourdough starter forever and bequeath it to your heirs. However, if it should ever develop an unusual appearance or odor, simply discard it and start anew.

SOURDOUGH FRENCH BREAD

Mix together in a large bowl 1 cup of sourdough starter with 1½ cups of warm water, ½ cup of vegetable oil, 2 tablespoons of honey or unsulfured molasses and about 6 cups of Cornell Mix (see pages 104–05). Blend all of the ingredients thoroughly by hand. Form into a ball, oil the surface and place it at the bottom of a large oiled bowl. Cover and store it in a warm room, away from drafts. Allow the dough to rise for several hours, until it has doubled in bulk. Remove 1 cupful of the dough and reserve it as the starter for the next baking. Then add 2 teaspoons of sea salt to the remaining dough. Knead the dough and shape it into 2 or 3 long loaves. Slip the loaves into oiled pans and allow them to rise for about 2 hours. Brush the tops with water and slash diagonal lines across them with a sharp knife. Bake in a preheated oven at 350° F. for 20 to 30 minutes, until golden brown and crisp. Makes 2 large, or 3 medium-size, loaves.

This recipe may be used for buns or rolls. Reduce the baking time, depending on the size of the buns or rolls.

SOURDOUGH PANCAKES

You will have to start the preparation for these pancakes the night before you plan to serve them, since the batter is raised overnight with baking yeast.

  1 tablespoon dried yeast granules (or 1 square of yeast)
  2 cups water lukewarm
1½ cups buckwheat flour
  ½ cup Cornell Mix (see pages 104–05)
  2 eggs, beaten
  ¾ teaspoon sea salt
  1 tablespoon unsulfured molasses
  1 cup sourdough starter

In the evening, soften the yeast in ½ cup of the water. Allow it to bubble and then add the remaining water. Stir in the buckwheat flour and Cornell Mix. Beat the batter and turn into a large pitcher, with enough empty space at the top so that the batter can rise without overflowing. Cover the pitcher and store at room temperature overnight. The next morning, stir down the batter and remove 1 cupful to store as the sourdough starter for the next batch. To the remaining batter add the eggs, salt, molasses and sourdough starter from the last batch. Mix well and pour onto a hot unoiled soapstone griddle (see Appendix) or into a heated oiled iron skillet. Brown lightly on both sides. Serve with fruit or cottage cheese. Serves 4 to 6, depending on the appetites.

Sourdough Starter and the Alaskan Gold Miners

Sourdough starter played a vital role in the gold-mining history of Alaska. The early miners were frequently called "Sourdoughs," and they were well acquainted with the value of this leavening.

It is hard for us to remember that food has not always been as close as the corner supermarket, or that it was ever hard to come by day to day. But the Alaskan gold miners had to wait for food supplies that—with luck—would come through once or twice a year. The necessities were transported by ship, then transferred to a smaller boat, a river steamer, a dog sled or even a backpack before they arrived. Because of sudden summer thaws, unusual ice formations, high winds or stormy seas, many supplies never reached their destination. Under these conditions, the men had to learn to husband whatever precious supplies they possessed until they could be certain that more supplies were coming.

So, to stretch the supplies, these men learned out of necessity to bake, creating many variations of hot breads, cakes, muffins and breads—when they were fortunate enough to have flour in the barrel. Baking requires leavening. At first, some of the men tried to carry baking yeast along with other supplies as they traveled northward. But yeast is perishable, and many a precious supply was deactivated by the bitter cold. Through trial and error, the men found a suitable leavener—tough and hearty as themselves—in sourdough starter.

Alaska abounds with stories about how old-timers struggled to keep their sourdough starter alive. In extremely cold weather the culture might be put under the blankets, protected by human warmth. On long journeys, some miners wore bags containing the precious sourdough starter inside their shirts. Treated thus almost as an amulet, the starter symbolized the struggle between life and death. When camp was broken, the starter was the very last thing to be placed in the pack sack, and was the first to be considered upon arrival at a new campsite.

Although the rigorous challenges that faced the old Alaskan Sourdoughs may not be with us today, we can still make sourdough starter as a leavening agent and enjoy the savory flavor and aroma it gives to all baked goods. Sourdough is a symbolic link that joins past, present and future.

Suggested Reading

Braué, John Rahn, *Uncle John's Original Bread Book*. New York: Exposition Press, 1965, "Sourdough," pp. 41–44.

Brown, Edward Espe, *The Tassajara Bread Book*. Berkeley, California: Shambala Publications, 1970, "Sourdough Bread and Pancakes," pp. 85–88.

Dworkin, Floss and Stan, *Bake Your Own Bread and Be Healthier*. New York: Holt, Rinehart and Winston, 1972. "Sourdough: Trapping the Wild Yeast," pp. 87–116.

Hunter, Beatrice Trum, *Fermented Foods and Beverages: An Old Tradition*. New Canaan, Connecticut: Keats Publishing, 1973, "Yeasts and Leaveners," pp. 103–108.

Sunnell, Agnes, *Sourdough*. College, Alaska: University of Alaska, Cooperative Extension Service, Publication No. 29, undated.

USDA publications:

"A Comeback for Convenience Bread?" *Agricultural Research*, August 1970.

"Wider Horizons for Sourdough." *Agricultural Research*, August 1969.

7 Sauerkraut

❦

Though you probably think of sauerkraut as a traditional German dish (*sauer* meaning acid or sour, and *kraut* meaning cabbage) the use of fermented cabbage probably originated in ancient China. As early as the third century B.C. this food sustained Chinese workers engaged in building that monumental project the Great Wall.

The Tartars carried sauerkraut westward. The Vikings, whose supply of fresh food was exhausted before the end of long voyages, wisely stored ample supplies of sauerkraut on their vessels before they left. James Lind, the noted eighteenth-century British surgeon, observed that Dutch ships carried huge barrels of *zourkool* to prevent scurvy among the sailors, a practice used long before the discovery that limes and lemons were antiscorbutic agents. Captain Cook carried thousands of pounds of cabbage on his ship to prevent the ravages of scurvy among his sailors.

Sauerkraut, and other fermented vegetables, were used extensively by our forefathers. Fermentation was one of several methods to preserve food for future use. Fermented vegetables such as sauerkraut also added variety to an otherwise monotonous diet.

Scientific investigations showed that sauerkraut gives us all the valuable nutrients of cabbage and furnishes them in a palatable and more easily digested form. Louis Pasteur described sauerkraut as one of the most useful and healthful of all vegetable dishes.

For those who grew up in nineteenth-century rural America or Europe, making sauerkraut was a common experience and it was not unusual for a single family to process hundreds of cabbage heads for sauerkraut. This autumn activity was as regular as pickling, jelly- and jam-making, drying, curing, smoking, or root-cellaring of foods. These items were—to borrow a nineteenth-century phrase covering such food preservation activities—"put by" to feed the family during the winter.

With today's supermarket offerings, you may not feel the urgency to "put by" foods. Nevertheless, there are reasons why you may want to make homemade sauerkraut. Today's commercial product is apt to be cooked, bleached with sulfur dioxide, preserved with benzoate of soda, and taste excessively salty—all features that make the product very different from homemade sauerkraut. Fortunately, sauerkraut is easy to make and requires no special ingredients, skills nor equipment. Nor do you need to gather hundreds of cabbage heads. Even a single head will do!

Salt for Sauerkraut Making

Traditionally, ordinary table salt has been used for sauerkraut as well as for dry-salting of other vegetables. But USDA reports that the anti-caking agents now added to salt (and listed on the label) are undesirable for sauerkraut making. USDA also advises against the use of coarse salt, such as the salt used for freezing ice cream; or of rock salt, which is likely to contain impurities.

USDA recommends finely textured salt for sauerkraut making, since it dissolves quickly and can be distributed evenly. The agency recommends three grades of salt for this purpose: granulated, flake (dairy) or medium. USDA adds that "if your grocery store does not carry any of these, you are likely to find them at a store selling feeds and garden supplies." The flake and medium grades of salt are more bulky than the granulated. By weight, it takes about 1½ cups of flake or medium salt to equal 1 cup of granulated salt.

I have found that both sea salt and earth salt, obtainable in health food stores or some special sections of supermarkets, are satisfactory for sauerkraut making. I have also discovered that kelp, which you can also buy in health-food stores, can be substituted for a portion of the salt. If you use kelp in part, the finished sauerkraut and its juice taste less salty. This is especially good for people who have learned to use *all* salts sparingly, by habit or because of medical restriction. Of course, any sauerkraut or sauerkraut juice at all may be *proscribed* for those on low-sodium diets.

Whichever salt you decide to use, measure it carefully. Too much salt prevents proper lactic-acid fermentation, and results in a poorly flavored sauerkraut. Too little salt makes an undesirably soft-textured sauerkraut, or can even interfere with fermentation.

Mix the salt evenly through the cabbage. Uneven distribution can be another factor in producing undesirably soft-textured sauerkraut.

Selecting and Preparing the Cabbage

Make sauerkraut from green or red head cabbage, or use a combination of both. For variety, try Chinese cabbage. It used to be that only late or fall head cabbage was considered suitable for sauerkraut, but you can make a good sauerkraut from cabbage maturing at any season of the year as long as you use sound, solid heads.

Remove the outer leaves, which would produce an off-color in the finished sauerkraut, and save them for soups or stews. Cut away any decayed or bruised portions. Remove the cores and grate them into salad.

Shred the cabbage with a shredding device or use a sharp knife to slice it as thin as you can. After all the cabbage is shredded, choose one of the following methods for making sauerkraut.

METHOD I: MAKING SAUERKRAUT IN
CANNING JARS

A quart-size screwtop canning jar will hold about 2 pounds of cabbage shreds. Weigh the shredded cabbage on a scale. Prepare the canning jars by washing and scalding them thoroughly. For each 2 pounds of shreds, sprinkle 4 level teaspoons of pure granulated salt (or 2 tablespoons of flake dairy or medium salt; or 2 tablespoons of sea or earth salt, or a mixture of these salts and kelp) over the shreds. Mix the shreds and salt together by hand. Pack this mixture into the jars, leaving some space at the top. Press down firmly, either with a wooden spoon or tamper. The salt will draw the juice from the cabbage and gradually form a brine. Continue pressing until enough brine forms to cover the cabbage. Cover the packed cabbage with a pad of plastic netting or cheesecloth. Over this, insert 2 pliable wood strips crosswise, so that they catch under the neck of the jar. This arrangement will keep the cabbage pressed down under the brine. Screw the lids on *loosely,* and set the packed jars in a shallow pan or on layers of newspapers. Store the jars at a fairly even temperature (around 70° F.) and from time to time check the fermentation process. The brine may overflow. If so, wipe the jars gently. If you have followed the directions carefully, scum should not form. After about 10 days, the brine level will drop rather suddenly, indicating that fermentation has finished. Remove the wooden strips and netting or cheesecloth. Make 2½ percent brine from 1 ounce of salt to each quart of water. Fill each jar with brine to within 1 inch of the top. Screw the lids tightly and either refrigerate or keep the jars in a cool pantry. This raw sauerkraut will keep for a few weeks. If you wish to store it indefinitely, either freeze or can it. To freeze, transfer the sauerkraut to freezer containers, filling them to within an inch of the top. To can, use a boiling water bath. Keep the sauerkraut in the same quart jars in which it has fermented. Press it down firmly with a spoon to release any gas bubbles. Fill the jars with brine—in the same proportions as above—to within ½ inch of the top and screw the lids on *loosely*. Lower the jars into a large vessel. Fill the vessel with water so that the tops of the jars are submerged. Boil the water for 20 minutes. Carefully remove the jars and place them in a shallow pan lined with a towel. Screw the tops tightly, allow them to cool, wipe clean, and store.

METHOD II: MAKING SAUERKRAUT IN A CROCK

Put the cabbage shreds in a large bowl. For every head of cabbage, add 3 level tablespoons of finely textured salt, or a combination of salt and kelp. Press the grated cabbage with your fingers, and allow the salt to draw out some liquid. Continue pressing for about 5 minutes. Turn the salted shreds and juice into a clean crock (or sound bowl with a good glaze). Press the mixture to the bottom and add enough brine (see page 131) to cover it well. Place several layers of plastic netting or cheesecloth on top to keep the shreds submerged. Choose a plate that is slightly smaller than the crock (or bowl), and place it on top of the netting or cheesecloth. Weight it with a few clean, heavy stones. Cover the crock or bowl and store it at room temperature. You will begin to smell the fermentation after a few days, and a scum will form on the top. Remove this scum daily with a small tea strainer or slotted spoon. If you do not remove the scum, it will destroy the desirable acid in the brine, as well as the sauerkraut itself. The fermentation is finished when the scum stops forming. This process will take a week or two, depending mainly on the room temperature. Remove the stones, plate and netting or cheesecloth, pack the sauerkraut into jars and cover it with the brine. Refrigerate this raw sauerkraut between 40° and 55° F; it will keep for a long time. Or you can freeze or can it, as described on page 132.

METHOD III: MAKING SAUERKRAUT BY ALTERNATE LAYERING

Instead of dissolving the salt in water to make a brine, as in Methods I and II, alternately layer the cabbage shreds and salt. This method may appear simpler than having to make a brine, but it is tricky for the novice. If you use too much salt in the bottom layering, you may run short on the top layering. Proper measuring will take some experience. Measure the cabbage shreds and salt; for each 5 pounds of cabbage shreds, use 3 tablespoons of salt, or a combination of salt and kelp. Pack a layer of shreds at the bottom of a crock or bowl. Strew a layer of salt on top. Add another layer of shreds and tamp it down to draw out the juices as well as to extract any trapped air. Repeat this layering, ending with a layer of salt. The top layer in the crock or bowl should be at the level where you will cover the mixture with netting or cheesecloth, plate and stones. If there is not enough juice pressed out to submerge the shreds, add a little water. Then proceed as in Method II.

VARIATIONS

In addition to shredding the cabbage, cut pieces of raw carrot, celery, onion, cauliflower, string beans, white or yellow turnip, and allow these raw vegetables to ferment along with the cabbage shreds. If you decide to add them, use Method II, since it is easier to add them to a crock or bowl than to the jars. These fermented vegetables are tasty additions.

To vary the flavoring of finished sauerkraut, add a few juniper berries. Or add some celery, caraway and/or dill seeds to the brine, using about a teaspoon for each head of cabbage. If you grind these seeds first in a seed grinder (see Appendix) their flavor will be stronger.

Using Sauerkraut

Sauerkraut is best used raw. It makes a piquant accompaniment for meat, fowl or seafoods. Or it can be a basic ingredient in a salad.

SAUERKRAUT SALAD

1 quart raw sauerkraut, drained
2 carrots, shredded
1 tablespoon parsley, minced
bed of crisp salad greens

Blend together the sauerkraut, carrots and parsley and turn the mixture onto the greens. Chill. It is unnecessary to add salad dressing. Serves 6.

WINTER SALAD

1 quart raw sauerkraut, drained
2 apples, unpeeled and sliced

Blend together. Chill. Serves 6.

SUMMER SALAD

This color combination is striking.

1 quart raw red cabbage sauerkraut, drained
3 avocadoes, cut in half
bed of crisp salad greens

Heap a portion of the sauerkraut into each avocado cavity. Arrange them on a bed of salad greens. Chill. Serves 6.

Using Sauerkraut Juice

Formerly, sauerkraut juice was considered as liquid "waste" and was generally discarded. In commercial production, out of every hundred tons of cabbage used for processing, about 20 tons of this brine leached from fermented cabbage was merely spewed into municipal sewerage systems or, more sensibly, spread on fields as fertilizer.

Scientists discovered that this discarded "waste" was nutrient-laden, especially with lactic acid. Now this piquant juice is processed and sold as sauerkraut juice, which has among other characteristics, a well-deserved reputation as a laxative.

When you make homemade sauerkraut, by all means plan to use the juice. Store the sauerkraut well covered in the juice. When you have finished eating the sauerkraut, save some of the brine and use it as a starter for your next batch of sauerkraut. Use it to replace some of the liquid, and you will discover that this brine speeds the fermentation.

Plan to drink some of it. Or, if you find it too salty, add it to cold summer soups, or mix it with other liquids to make refreshing appetizers.

SAUERKRAUT JUICE DRINK

2 cups raw sauerkraut juice
2 cups apple juice, unsweetened

Blend together and chill. Serves 6.

BLUSHING PINK APPETIZER

2 cups raw red cabbage sauerkraut juice
2 cups tomato or V-8 juice
½ cup yogurt or sour cream

Blend all ingredients together in an electric blender. Chill. Serves 6.

Sauerkraut Science and Technology

Workers at the Agricultural Experiment Station at Geneva, New York, have been concerned with sauerkraut production for half a century. They have been dealing with such problems as spoilage, quality control and pollution from sauerkraut production. This agency, located in the "sauerkraut capital of America" in the upper part of the state, has helped turn sauerkraut making from a home activity into a large-scale commercial production. It appears that the fruits of their work can still benefit you, the home producer of sauerkraut, as well as the large food processors.

Six years ago, a plant breeder at the Geneva Station began to breed cabbages to increase their dry-matter content, and reduce the water content that eventually becomes brine. He conducted extensive experiments, crossing ordinary cabbage with savoy cabbage, which has a loose, dry head; with Brussels sprouts; and with kale. The result was cabbage which should reduce brine production by half, while still keeping other desirable characteristics including large, firm round cabbage heads that mature uniformly and are disease-resistant. The newly bred cabbage is called "Hi-Dri Kraut," and its seeds have been distributed to seed companies by the Geneva Station. (As of 1973 the seeds of "Hi-Dri Kraut" cabbage were not yet available for vegetable gardeners. The Department of Vegetable Crops of the Geneva Station reports that it will be several years before the seed companies will have increased the seeds of this cabbage sufficiently to be able to make it available for sale.)

Food technologists concerned with processing sauerkraut have been less successful than the plant breeders. Technologists have been studying the merits of using dehydration, freeze-drying and microwave dehydration to process sauerkraut. To date, they have not had any success with these processing techniques, which are vastly inferior to the traditional methods. Sauerkraut dehydrated by conventional hot air became shrunken and dark. Freeze-dried sauerkraut was comparable to, but not superior to, the canned commercial product. Microwave dehydration caused extreme browning and a considerable loss of ascorbic acid in some samples. To make sauerkraut, the best method still seems to be the time-honored, natural fermentation process used by our forefathers. Perhaps there is a moral here for food technologists eager to "improve" on nature in food processing.

Suggested Reading

Brody, Jane E., "Upstate Town Is Sauerkraut Capital, Where Science Attacks Old Problems." *The New York Times,* May 29, 1973.
Hertzberg, Ruth, Vaughan, Beatrice, and Greene, Janet, *Putting Foods By.* Brattleboro, Vermont: Stephen Greene Press, 1973, pp. 95, 299.
Hunter, Beatrice Trum, *Fermented Foods and Beverages: An Old Tradition.* New Canaan, Connecticut: Keats Publishing, 1973, pp. 15–17.
Hunter, Beatrice Trum, *The Natural Foods Cookbook.* New York: Simon and Schuster, 1961, "Homemade Sauerkraut," pp. 261–262.
Stoner, Carol, editor, *Stocking Up: How to Preserve the Foods You Grow, Naturally.* Emmaus, Pennsylvania: Rodale Press, 1973.
USDA publications:
Preservation of Vegetables by Fermentation and Salting, Farmers' Bulletin No. 881, August 1917.
Preservation of Vegetables by Salting or Brining, Farmers' Bulletin No. 1932, June 1944.
"Research on Sauerkraut." *USDA's Service,* December 1939, page 3.

8 Yogurt

✤

"Yourt," "Yohourt," "Yohurti," and "Yogurt" are only a few variations on the name of this popular cultured-milk product, which has been known at least since Biblical times. Yogurt has long been a staple food in Lebanon, Syria, Bulgaria, Yugoslavia and India. In recent years, yogurt has become popular in the United States, where, in the last decade, sales have jumped 500 percent. Unfortunately, some of this increased popularity stems from overenthusiasm and advertising puffery, which attribute some doubtful properties to yogurt. Among some of the false notions are that yogurt will correct overweight, restore hair, tone up flaccid muscles and increase sexual prowess for senior citizens. Currently, these claims have caused yogurt to be exploited rather weirdly at times—for example, used along with strawberries in a hair shampoo, or in another case in a quantity of 200 pounds used in a beauty bath by a publicity-seeking model.

Although yogurt is neither a panacea nor an elixir, certain properties make it superior to the plain milk from which it is made. Yogurt develops somewhat different food values than those found in sweet milk. In addition to the possibility that some vitamins, notably vitamin B, are synthesized by the bacteria in the fermented milk, yogurt offers at least four different health benefits not offered by the sweet milk from which it is made: (1) its bactericidal powers against pathogens; (2) its alleviation of many gastrointestinal distresses; (3) its restoration of beneficial flora in the intestinal tract which have been destroyed by antibiotic medication; and (4) its greater digestibility than sweet milk by persons who have any degree of lactose intolerance.

Preparing Yogurt at Home

Traditionally, yogurt has been made at home. "No one made richer, smoother yogurt than my Little Aunt of blessed memory," reminisced Turkish-born Selma. Her Little Aunt would finish her chores and then turn to the yogurt-making ritual. A special room was reserved for this, and she usually worked alone and undisturbed. When Selma was privileged to enter, she noticed that the small tidy room contained a wooden box filled with straw. Nearby, numerous old blankets were piled neatly on a shelf. Rows of earthenware bowls lined the counter. Little Aunt poured the milk into a pot reserved especially for heating it. When the milk came to a boil, she would remove it from the heat.

"Rule number one," Little Aunt would say, "never overboil the milk, or the yogurt will have a bad taste."

Then Little Aunt would pour the hot milk into the bowls and allow it to cool. That, Selma was told, was rule number two. Impatiently Selma would ask Little Aunt how she knew when the milk was cool enough.

Little Aunt would demonstrate as she said, "I put my little finger into the milk. If it does not burn me, I know it is ready." When Little Aunt was satisfied that the temperature was correct, she would add a spoonful of yogurt she had kept from the previous day's batch. Then she would carry the bowls to the box, set them inside, pile straw around them, place the cover carefully, and lay the blankets on top.

"Rule number three," Little Aunt would announce, while arranging the blankets and tucking in their edges, "the place has to be warm. Otherwise the yogurt will not set." On cold days, as an added precaution, Little Aunt instructed that the box be carried into the living room and placed near the coal stove.

Little Aunt would check on the yogurt by lifting the covers carefully and peering inside. Invariably her face would break into a radiant smile as she would announce with pleasure in her voice that the yogurt was ready.

"Somehow, no yogurt tasted as good as the kind my Little Aunt prepared with care and love, and served with pride when we all gathered around the big dining-room table," recalled Selma nostalgically.

Through the centuries, many people have prepared homemade yogurt using techniques similar to Little Aunt's. Basically, there are always three steps: (1) heating the milk; (2) culturing it; and (3) incubating it until yogurt is formed. Through the centuries, the strains of culture were not always pure, the heating and cooling of the milk was not highly accurate, and absolute control of the incubating temperature was impossible. Despite these obstacles, superb yogurt was made and enjoyed.

Although the basic techniques remain the same, modern technology has made it possible to keep the strains of yogurt culture pure; the temperature, even; and, with the use of equipment such as dairy thermometers and stainless steel vessels, the quality controlled. Such features are extremely useful for commercial yogurt-making, and though they can serve in making homemade yogurt, they are not essential for the homemade product.

Although good commercial yogurt is sold, it is unobtainable in some areas. If you prefer to make yogurt at home, you will find that there are advantages. You can make your own yogurt inexpensively, and make it as mild or as tart as you like. You can make and eat it fresh, without guesswork about its age. (Commercial yogurt is often sold undated.) You can enjoy it plain or flavored; if you do decide to flavor it, you can use naturally sweet fresh fruits and honey, and omit the sugar or sugar-laden ingredients.

Milk for Yogurt Making

Almost any type of milk will turn to yogurt successfully. The milk is the vehicle for the culture. It can be raw, pasteurized, homogenized, or low-fat; from animals such as cows, goats, mares, sheep, buffalo; or from a plant source such as soybeans. The milk should be fresh. The older the milk, the longer it will take to incubate, or the more starter it will require.

If you have access to clean raw milk, morning milk is reported to produce the best-flavored yogurt. You will have to pasteurize raw milk for yogurt-making, in order to kill other bacteria possibly present which would interfere with the *Lactobacilli*, the bacteria responsible for culturing yogurt.

If you plan to use low-fat milk, read the label carefully. Sometimes thickening or bodying agents are added to overcome the "skinny" mouth feel of low-fat milk. These agents, such as cornstarch, tapioca or chemical emulsifiers, will interfere with the culturing of yogurt.

Sometimes, through no fault of yours, yogurt will not form. A farmer using penicillin as medication for a cow is legally required to withhold the milk from the market until the penicillin residue no longer appears in the milk. However, this procedure is not always followed and penicillin residue interferes with the culturing of yogurt (and cheese). At times this problem has been so widespread that factories have had to discontinue cheese and yogurt production because they could not obtain regular supplies of penicillin-free milk.

Do not use canned condensed milk for yogurt-making as it is presweetened; and, although canned evaporated milk makes yogurt successfully, there is at present a reason why its use cannot be recommended. Canned milk products are processed in containers made by a century-old soldering technique which may contaminate canned milk with residues of poisonous lead, tin and cadmium. Newer canning techniques *could* be used which would eliminate these hazards, but they have not yet been instituted.

Starter for Yogurt-Making

If you are making yogurt at home for the first time, obtain a good-quality fresh starter. This may be a special starter supplied with a commercial yogurt incubator; a special starter sold through the mail or at health-food stores (these tend to be expensive); a small amount of yogurt from a friend or neighbor who makes yogurt regularly (gratis); or a small amount of yogurt from fresh commercial yogurt (inexpensive). Be sure to use only plain, unflavored yogurt as a starter.

If, after making many batches of yogurt you notice that the product appears weakened in appearance or taste, renew the starter, or boost it with some additional fresh starter.

Containers for Yogurt-Making

A variety of containers commonly found at home can be used for successful yogurt-making. Choose containers of inert material, such as widemouthed glass canning or freezing jars, ovenproof glass or crockery custard cups, earthenware bowls, stone crocks or casseroles. They should be sound, without cracks, crazes or poor glazes.

If the containers lack lids, improvise. For example, plastic lids from some cans of peanuts or coffee snap tightly over flare-rimmed custard cups and form a tight seal. Or cut lids from circles of brown or parchment paper, or aluminum foil and hold them in place with rubber bands or strings.

Incubators for Yogurt-Making

The large number of commercially available yogurt incubators now being sold for home use confirms the popularity of homemade yogurt. Some of these devices rely on electricity, while a few do not. If you decide to purchase and use one of these commercial incubators, follow the directions given.

However, a commercial yogurt incubator is nonessential. Numerous pieces of commonly available equipment in your home will allow you to devise your own yogurt incubator. Approach yogurt-making with a sense of adventure. Explore various possible incubating equipment, and choose a method that works well for *you*. The following are some of the inexpensive and ingenious incubators that persons have used successfully. Obviously, there is a wealth of possibilities.

Polystyrene ice bucket or *picnic hamper:* If you plan to make only a small quantity of yogurt in small jars, the former is satisfactory; for a larger amount, the latter is preferable. Both are inexpensive.

Electric hot tray or *electric food warmer:* Test these devices by placing a covered bowl, filled with warm water, on top of either, and keep it there for a few hours. If the temperature can be maintained at about 110° F. the tray or warmer will be suitable as a yogurt incubator.

Electric heating pad: Turn to the lowest heat, and insert at the bottom of an insulated bag. Wrap the jars in towels and place them in the bag.

Electric skillet: Turn to the lowest heat. Set the jars in the skillet, standing in warm water. Maintain the water at a low, even heat.

Oven of electric stove: Turn the heat to 120° F. and then turn it off. Allow the oven to cool to 90° F. and while the yogurt incubates in the oven, try to keep the oven temperature between 90° and 105° F. You may need to do some frequent checking. If the temperature needs to be raised, turn the oven heat on briefly, with the door slightly ajar, but without disturbing the incubating yogurt jars.

Iron pot containing warm water: Lower the jars of incubating yogurt into the pot and cover them with a blanket. Check the temperature of the water from time to time and reheat if necessary. The iron pot retains heat well.

Gentle heat source: This may be the pilot light on top of a gas stove, a steam-heat radiator, a hot-air floor register, a heating duct, a banked woodstove fire, a warm area at the back of the refrigerator, or even on top of a TV set in use! After you have located a gentle heat source, place the incubating yogurt over it and wrap the jars.

Wide-mouthed thermos: Allow the milk to incubate in the closed thermos, which will retain the steady heat required for the length of time necessary to culture the yogurt. If you use this method, in order to avoid breakage stir the culture into the cooling milk in another container before pouring it into the thermos.

Old-fashioned featherbed or comforter: Use either of these natural insulators, or a warm blanket, to wrap around the jars of incubating yogurt.

Old-fashioned "fireless cooker": T. W. Fowle has kindly supplied the following directions. For a family-sized batch, make a corrugated paperboard box 7 inches high by 7 to 8 inches square, enough space for 4 tall peanut-butter jars. Quart-size jars require a box at least 8 inches square. Tuck thick folded huck towels over and around the jars. Then cover the box completely with a heavy blanket. Place this small box into a larger one, 12 by 12 inches, and 15 inches high. Insulate between both boxes at the bottom, top, and sides, by using clean cotton rags, shredded paper, or cotton batting. Bend the top flaps of the smaller box downward, so that they can be tucked into the larger box, and provide additional insulation at the sides. Place a pillow on top, so that the inside box is completely covered. Close the top of the outside box, and hold it in place with heavy cord. A piece of plywood placed under the cord will help keep the top flat and closed and protect the box from being cut by the string.

Old-fashioned "hay box": This is similar to the box used by Selma's Turkish Little Aunt (see page 140). Place a small wooden box inside of a larger one. For insulation, fill the spaces between with clean hay. Or, use vermiculite, sawdust, wood shavings, feathers, polystyrene chips or bubbles. All of these materials are good insulators, but be careful to keep them from contaminating the incubating yogurt.

The ideal temperature for incubating yogurt is within the range of 105° and 112° F. for several hours. You can control the degree of tartness. The faster you can culture the milk, the milder will be its taste; the longer, the tarter.

PREPARING THE YOGURT

To make 1 quart of yogurt, measure a quart of milk into a scrupulously clean saucepan. If you like thick yogurt, add 2 tablespoons of milk powder for each quart of milk, and dissolve it while the milk is still cold. Cover the pot and gradually bring the milk to the simmer point. If you use medium heat, this will require about 20 minutes. Remove the simmering milk from the heat and pour it into 2 clean, heat-resistant scalded pint jars, or into several scalded custard cups, or whatever containers you plan to use. Allow the milk to cool for about 7 minutes. This slight cooling is necessary in order not to kill the culture with excessive heat.

Then, it is ready to be cultured. Add the starter, using only about a tablespoon of it for each quart of milk. If you add too much, the yogurt will have an unpleasant grainy texture. Stir the culture into the milk. If you don't, you may finish with a quart of cooled milk and a glob of yogurt at the bottom of the containers. Cover the jars and place them in whatever incubating device you have chosen to use.

If you are using the polystyrene picnic hamper—one of my favorite incubators because of its cheapness, accessibility and reliability—pour enough warm water into the bottom of the hamper so that the water level reaches the shoulder of the jars. Set the jars in the water and cover the hamper tightly. Allow the jars to rest undisturbed for a few hours. Then check them by gently tilting one jar slightly. If the milk is still thin and runny, put it back into the hamper. But if the milk has begun to thicken, even slightly, remove the jars, wipe dry, and refrigerate them. The yogurt will continue to thicken in the refrigerator. Yogurt stores best between 35° and 45° F. Within 24 hours after refrigeration, the yogurt will be ready to eat.

The culturing milk should neither be overincubated nor underincubated. To avoid overincubation, plan to make yogurt during the day rather than culturing it overnight. Overincubation toughens the curd. This is especially undesirable if you plan to strain yogurt and feed it to a baby from a bottle.

If you allow the culturing milk to become too cool during the incubation, you will retard the growth of bacteria responsible for culturing the yogurt. If this happens, increase the temperature, incubate longer and, if necessary, add a little more starter.

If you have allowed the milk to become too hot (above 115° F.) you will have killed off the yogurt-making bacteria. Even though this milk will no longer make yogurt, you need not discard it. Use it as the base for a creamed vegetable soup, a milk drink, a baked custard; or turn it into cottage cheese.

Using Yogurt

The cultured yogurt, refrigerated for 24 hours, is ready to eat. If there is any watery separation on top, it is merely nutritious whey. Never attempt to stir the whey back into the yogurt. This movement only causes further separation and it is a sign that you are a yogurt novice. Your action will provoke glares from a true yogurt aficionado. To minimize the separation, use a wooden spoon or some other lightweight implement to scoop yogurt out of the container.

Although refrigerated yogurt will keep for a long time, it is best eaten within a week's time, when the bactericidal value is highest. If you wish to flavor the yogurt, add the flavor to the finished product, but remember to save some plain yogurt for culturing the next batch.

Use yogurt in its natural state or with other foods. Dab it on top of baked potato or apple. Spoon it over cooked vegetables or stewed fruits. Use it as an ingredient in salads or appetizers; as a garnish for hot or cold soups or casseroles; or as a marinade for meat or fowl.

If you don't like plain yogurt, try flavoring it with one of these:

cinnamon, nutmeg, unsulfured molasses, honey, carob, pure vanilla or almond extract. Or, top yogurt with ground nuts, sesame seeds or wheat germ. If you object to the tartness of yogurt, add soaked dried fruits, berries or melon balls.

YOGURT COOLER

1 quart yogurt
juice of 1 lemon
juice of 2 oranges
2 tablespoons honey

Blend all ingredients together in an electric blender until smooth. Chill. Serves 6.

YOGURT-AVOCADO DIP

1 cup yogurt
2 avocados
1 clove of garlic
3 tablespoons chive, minced

Blend all ingredients together in an electric blender until smooth. Chill. Serve with thin rounds of raw white turnip. Makes 1 pint.

YOGURT SUMMER SOUP

2 cups yogurt
3 cucumbers, peeled, seeds removed, chopped
juice of 1 lemon or lime
1 tablespoon mint leaves

Blend all ingredients together in an electric blender until smooth. Chill for at least an hour to allow the mint to flavor the soup. Serves 6.

YOGURT VEGETABLE SAUCE

2 cups yogurt
1 tablespoon curry
1 tablespoon sweet paprika

Blend all ingredients together until smooth. Serve at room temperature over vegetables such as string beans, zucchini, cauliflower or broccoli. Makes 1 pint.

YOGURT APPLE WHIP

1½ cups applesauce, unsweetened
1½ cups yogurt
⅛ teaspoon cinnamon

Blend all ingredients together until smooth. Turn into 6 sherbet glasses. Chill. Serves 6.

If you use yogurt in cooking, allow it to stand at room temperature, then stir or fold it into other ingredients gradually and gently, using low heat. The custardlike texture of yogurt breaks down with vigorous beating. When cooked, yogurt thins out more than sour cream. You can stabilize yogurt with arrowroot starch. Mix the arrowroot starch with cold yogurt until it is dissolved, and then gradually add it to the heated mixture. Often you can substitute yogurt for buttermilk or sour cream in recipes; yogurt contains fewer calories than sour cream.

Learning to Like Yogurt

Not everyone likes yogurt the first time they sample it. Some people admit that they had to cultivate a taste for it. If you would like to use yogurt, but it doesn't yet appeal to you, the following advice will be heartening.

The late consulting nutritionist Dr. Michael J. Walsh was asked by someone how a person could cultivate a liking for buttermilk. Although Dr. Walsh's reply concerned buttermilk, the advice is equally applicable to yogurt.

Dr. Walsh replied: "The same procedure can be used for learning to like any food. First of all, bear in mind that no human has yet been born with a liking for, or a distaste for, any food, thing, or person. The like or the dislike has been acquired by a conditioning process. In other words, other than a relatively few unconditional reflexes, which include salivation at the taste of food, everything we know we have learned—so here is the conditioning mechanism for learning to like buttermilk.

"Make a point to take one ounce (one jigger) and only one ounce of buttermilk *once* a day, every day, for one week. During the second week, take one ounce *twice* a day, every day. During the third week, take one ounce *three* times a day, every day. During the fourth week, take two ounces three times a day, every day. By the sixth week, when you are taking four ounces of buttermilk three times a day, you have not only learned to like it, but you are likely to be licking your chops in relish as well as having already experienced the beneficial values of it. You understand now why I have no concern for those individuals who insist that they do not like this, they do not like that, they have a natural craving for sweets. Let me repeat—you can learn to like any food, or any person, if you choose to. Similarly, you can readily wean yourself away from foods like sweets, which you know are not good for you in the sense that they do not contribute to your well-being."

Suggested Reading

Alston, Elizabeth, "Yogurt—Fad or First-Rate Food?" *Family Health,* May 1972, p. 22.

Cooney, John E., "Oh, No, Not Yogurt! Many People Hate It, Yet Many Now Eat It." *Wall Street Journal,* March 28, 1972, p. 1.

"Cultured Dairy Foods." *Dairy Council Digest,* Vol. 43, No. 4, July–August 1972.

Ekrem, Selma, "Little Aunt's Yogurt." *Christian Science Monitor,* May 4, 1970.

How to Make Yogurt. USDA Agricultural Research Service, Dairy Products Laboratory, Publication Ca-E-15, 1967.

Hunter, Beatrice Trum, *The Natural Foods Cookbook.* New York: Simon and Schuster, 1961, "Homemade Yogurt," pp. 204–6.

Hunter, Beatrice Trum, *Yogurt, Kefir and Other Milk Cultures.* New Canaan, Connecticut: Keats Publishing, 1973.

Parker, Dorothy, *The Wonderful World of Yogurt.* New York: Hawthorn Books, 1972.

Peters, Joan, *Yogurt: Recipes for You and Your Family.* Durham, New Hampshire: Cooperative Extension Service, University of New Hampshire, 1973.

Shea, Kevin P., "Canned Milk." *Environment,* Vol. 15, No. 2, March 1972, pp. 6–11.

Smetinoff, Olga, *The Yogurt Cookbook.* New York: Frederick Fell, 1966.

Stoner, Carol, editor, *Stocking Up: How to Preserve the Foods You Grow, Naturally.* Emmaus, Pennsylvania: Rodale Press, 1973.

Thompson, Leona W., *Foods from Fermentation; Natural Foods.* Burlington, Vermont: Cooperative Extension Service, University of Vermont, Brieflet No. 38, 1972.

Walsh, Michael J., "Answers to Your Questions on Foods and Nutrition." *Modern Nutrition,* October 1963, p. 8.

9 Soybeans

❧

Meet the humble soybean. This little bean has been used for centuries in the Orient, where it has served as meat, milk, cheese, bread, oil and condiment. It is time to become better acquainted with this versatile legume.

As long ago as 2838 B.C. a Chinese emperor discussed the soybean in a book about plants of his country. The soybean has had a long use in China, Korea and Japan. When Buddhism was established and meat was excluded from the diet of Buddhists, the use of the soybean and fermented soybean products became widespread. Today, food fermentations in the Orient are spoken about as the "traditional food fermentations." These early pioneering efforts in the Orient have contributed greatly to our present knowledge of enzyme fermentation and flavoring agents.

Although you may associate the soybean with the Orient, what may be surprising is to learn that the soybean has been consumed there mainly in fermented form. From experience, many Orientals consider fermented soybeans more palatable and digestible than unfermented ones. In addition, fermented soybean products have added variety and flavor to the basic diet. In this form, foods keep well without spoilage. Furthermore, some fermentations from soybeans produce natural antibiotics.

You can use the soybean in many ways, both as foods and beverages. You can prepare some of them at home, and buy others at specialty stores.

Soybean Sprouts

If you have a vegetable garden, you can grow soybeans easily. If you intend to use the soybean crop for sprouting, any variety that germinates readily can be used, but field varieties have certain advantages. The beans, being small, produce the best sprouts. Also, since they germinate readily, they are not apt to spoil. Some gardeners prefer to plant black soybeans, for the sprouts are more tender. Others do not like the appearance of the dark seed coat, and prefer the crispness of lighter-colored varieties. Chief, Ebony, Illini, Lincoln and Richland are varieties considered to be good for sprouting purposes, Lincoln does especially well, producing long, attractive sprouts.

Although all raw soybeans have certain undesirable factors, these are largely inactivated by sprouting or by cooking. To sprout soybeans, follow the general directions for sprouting (see pages 70–71). Exercise care in sprouting soybeans. They are sometimes difficult to sprout in warm weather, or they mold easily. Refrigerate the soybeans when you soak them initially. Then add one-half teaspoon of chlorinated lime to a gallon of water and use this solution for the initial rinsing of the sprouts. Use soybean sprouts when the sprout is two inches long. Soybean sprouts will lose their beany flavor if you sauté them briefly.

Fresh Green Soybeans as a Vegetable

If you grow soybeans you can use a portion of them as a fresh vegetable, cooked like fresh lima beans. Freeze, can or dry any surplus for future use.

FREEZING FRESH GREEN SOYBEANS

Freezing is the best method of preserving fresh soybeans. The most satisfactory varieties for freezing are Funk Delicious, Hokkaido, Jugun, Willomi, Emperor, Green Giant, Imperial and Bansei. Select only young green beans of the best quality for freezing and process them as soon as you can after harvesting them. Blanch the unhulled beans, using 1½ quarts of water for every pound of soybeans. Pour the beans into rapidly boiling water, and, letting the water continue to boil vigorously, keep them there for exactly 5 minutes. Then thoroughly cool the beans by running cold water through them, hull, and pack them into freezer containers. Freeze them promptly and store at 0° F. or lower. When you wish to use frozen soybeans, place them frozen in a small quantity of boiling liquid (¾ cup of liquid for each pint of beans). Allow the liquid to return to a boil, and cook the beans from 10 to 12 minutes. Use these beans in the same way as cooked fresh soybeans.

CANNING FRESH GREEN SOYBEANS

If you can fresh soybeans you will destroy their brilliant green color and crisp texture. The canned beans will be quite soft and have a stronger flavor than the fresh ones. However, you may wish to can them, especially if you lack a freezer.

Select young beans for canning, choosing a variety that has small beans with a mild flavor. The larger beans will not be as good, as the beans form a thick jellied mass that causes the canning liquid to become cloudy.

Plan to can the soybeans immediately after you pick them. This practice will help to retain some of the natural sweetness of the bean. Even so, you may wish to add a little honey to counteract the change in flavor that inevitably results from canning. Use ½ to 1 teaspoon of honey per pint of soybeans.

You will need to hull the soybeans before you process them. In preparing them for freezing, the hulls come off quickly when they are blanched in boiling water. To make hulling easier for canning, pour boiling water over the soybeans and allow them to soak for 5 minutes. Drain the beans, cool and then hull them.

Boil the hulled soybeans for 3 to 4 minutes. While they are still hot, pack them into sterilized canning jars. Add the honey (proportions given above) plus ½ teaspoon of sea salt to each pint jar. Then cover the contents with boiling water. Although you can use the same water that you used for precooking the beans, the flavor will be strong. Place the jars, with their covers on, in a pressure cooker and process them: pint- or quart-size jars (No. 2, 2½ and 3 cans) for 1 hour, with 10 pounds of pressure.

When you open the cans for use, take the same precautions against possible botulism that you would take with all low-acid home-canned vegetables—that is, boil the soybeans for 10 minutes in an uncovered pan *before tasting them.*

DRYING FRESH GREEN SOYBEANS

Drying is the least desirable way of preserving green soybeans. However, there may be reasons why you wish to dry beans, especially if you lack both a freezer and a pressure cooker. Although dried soybeans will retain their green color quite well, they develop a strong, grassy flavor.

To dry soybeans, wash and blanch them in the pods by steaming them for 7 to 8 minutes. Blanch only a small quantity at a time, so that each pod will be exposed to the steam. Hull the beans and dry them in an oven (or a dehydrator) at 150° F. for the first half of the drying period, and then reduce the temperature to 145° F. for the remainder of the drying period. The entire drying process will take approximately 6 to 9 hours. The dried beans should be hard and wrinkled, but should retain their greenness.

As soon as the beans cool to room temperature, place them in airtight jars or moisture-proof bags and seal them completely. Store them in a cool, dry, dark place. In choosing the storage containers, if possible use those that are small enough to hold only the quantity of soybeans you will wish to use at one time. If you do this, you will avoid having to open and reseal containers repeatedly.

Whether you dry your own soybeans or buy them dry, prepare them for table use by rinsing and then soaking them in hot liquid for ½ hour. For each cup of beans, use 2½ cups of hot liquid. After they are soaked and reconstituted, simmer them gently for 10 minutes. Drain, season and serve them.

You can make a number of dishes from cooked soybeans. One of the most popular is baked soybeans, a dish similar to Boston baked beans. However, soybeans retain their crispness. The seasonings add some zip to soybeans which are quite bland.

BAKED SOYBEANS

4 cups soybeans, cooked and drained
1 teaspoon sea salt
3 tablespoons unsulfured molasses
1 cup tomato purée
1 onion, chopped fine
1 teaspoon curry powder

Combine all ingredients thoroughly and turn the mixture into a casserole. Cover and bake in a moderate oven (350° F.) for 2 hours. Serves 6.

SOYBEAN TOMATO ASPIC

1 tablespoon gelatin, unflavored
2 cups tomato juice
¼ teaspoon sea salt
1 teaspoon celery seed
1 onion, sliced
1 tablespoon parsley, minced
1 cup soybeans, cooked and drained
½ cup celery, chopped

Soak gelatin in ¼ cup of cold tomato juice. Heat the remainder of the tomato juice, with salt and celery seed, to the simmer point. Strain, add to soaked gelatin, and stir until it is dissolved. When slightly cool, add remaining ingredients and turn into a mold which has been rinsed first with cold water. Chill until firm. Unmold to serve. Serves 6.

MAKING SOYBEAN PULP

To make soybean pulp, put cooked, drained soybeans through a meat grinder. One cup of cooked soybeans will make about 1½ cups of lightly packed pulp.

GREEN PEPPERS STUFFED WITH
SOYBEAN PULP

  6 large green peppers
 1½ cups soybean pulp
  2 eggs
 ⅓ cup celery, diced
  1 small onion, minced
  1 tablespoon nuts, ground

Remove seeds and inner partitions from green peppers. Fill the cavities with a mixture of the soybean pulp, eggs, celery and onions. Cover the tops with the nuts. Arrange green peppers so that they stand in an oiled pan. Bake in a hot oven (400° F.) for ½ hour, or until the peppers are soft. Serves 6.

ROASTING DRY SOYBEANS

To roast soybeans, soak dry soybeans overnight in the refrigerator. The next day drain and dry them between towels. Spread them out in shallow pans and dry them further for about 2 hours in a low oven (200° F.). When the soybeans are quite dry, place them under the broiler. Shake the pans constantly to prevent them from burning. Allow them to become golden brown and remove any that may have burned. These roasted soybeans can be eaten as they are, or oiled and seasoned. Keep them whole, to use as a snack, or grind them to use as nut substitutes.

MAKING SOYBEAN MILK

"Soybean milk" is a term applied to various preparations, but it is simply a water extract from dry beans. This extract contains salts, sugars, protein and some of the fat of the original soybeans. To extract soybean milk, wash 1 pound of dry soybeans and soak them in 2 quarts of cold water. Refrigerate them overnight. Drain the beans and, using the finest attachment of a food grinder, grind them. Put the ground beans into a cheesecloth bag and place this pulp in a pan containing 2 quarts of lukewarm water. Using your hands, work the pulp thoroughly for 10 minutes. Then wring the bag out over the pan and remove it. Whatever liquid has flowed through the bag into the pan is the "soybean milk." Boil it for 10 minutes, stirring frequently, then cool and refrigerate it.

Soybean milk can be substituted for cow's milk in many recipes, but they are different both in composition and flavor. Soybean milk is especially useful in the diet of individuals, particularly infants, who are allergic to cow's milk. But some individuals are allergic to soybean milk and other soybean products, notably soy bakery products.

If you use soybean milk in cooking, use it in the same proportions as cow's milk in recipes. Soybean milk, like milk from animals, is perishable and will sour. To store, refrigerate it.

SPICED SOYBEAN MILK

1 quart soybean milk
¼ teaspoon ginger, ground
¼ teaspoon nutmeg, ground
⅓ cup unsulfured molasses

Blend all ingredients together in an electric blender. Chill. Serves 6.

RICE PUDDING WITH SOYBEAN MILK

2 cups brown rice, cooked
1 cup soybean milk
3 tablespoons honey
1 apple, chopped fine
1 teaspoon cinnamon
⅓ cup raisins

Blend all ingredients together and turn the mixture into 6 buttered custard cups. Bake in a moderate oven (350° F.) for about 40 minutes or until the pudding is set and golden brown on top. Serves 6.

MAKING SOYBEAN CURD

Soybean curd, "soybean cheese," or "tofu" are familiar to many Westerners as well as to Easterners. Soybean curd can be made at home from soybean milk, soybean flour, the soybeans themselves, or from fermented soybean milk. It can be used as cheese, or it can be blended into various dishes. Soybean curd looks like cream cheese but it has a stronger flavor. It is easily digested.

To make soybean curd from soybean milk, heat a quart of soybean milk to 180° F. Remove it from the heat source, add 1 cup of apple-cider vinegar and stir the mixture well. The vinegar will curdle the soybean milk. Let it stand for a few minutes and then pour it into a cheesecloth bag. Dip the bag into cold water several times to wash away the excess acid. Drain the bag for an hour, and then press out the remaining liquid. Season the curd with sea salt and pack it tightly into a dampened mold, consisting of a topless and bottomless wooden box which has been placed on a flat tray or plate. Place a weight on top. Cover the mold and refrigerate until the soybean curd is firm enough to cut. Like cottage cheese, soybean curd is perishable. To store, wrap in cheesecloth, place in a bowl, cover with cold water and refrigerate.

To make soybean curd from fermented soybean milk, keep the sweet soybean milk in a warm place overnight, or until it forms a curd naturally. Break the curd by stirring, and add an equal quantity of water heated to a near-boil. Allow the mixture to stand for 10 minutes. Then pour it into a cheesecloth bag, and proceed as above.

To make soybean curd from soybean flour, beat 1 cup of full-fat soybean flour into 1 cup of cold water until it forms a smooth paste. Add the paste to another cup of boiling water and cook it for 5 minutes. Remove it from the heat source and add ½ cup of apple-cider vinegar. Allow the mixture to cool. When it coagulates, strain it through the cheesecloth and proceed as above.

To make soybean curd from soybeans, soak 1 cup of dry soybeans in 3 cups of cold water and refrigerate overnight. In the morning, discard the water and rinse the soybeans with fresh cold water. Drain and grind them in a meat grinder. Or grind them in an electric blender with a little water to form a paste. Measure the paste, turn it into a pot and add 3 times as much water as paste. Mix and heat to the simmer point. Remove the pot from the heat source and add ½ cup of apple-cider vinegar. When the mixture coagulates, strain it through the cheesecloth and proceed as above.

Using Soybean Flours

Soybean flours are not true flours in the sense that wheat or rye are. Soybean flours do not contain any gluten, which binds dough together for baking purposes. They do not contain any of the starch that thickens sauces.

It is better to think of soybean flours as highly concentrated vegetable protein foods comparable to other concentrated foods such as milk powder or powdered eggs.

There are three types of soybean flours.

High-fat or *full-fat soybean flour:* This flour comes from ground-up soybeans with nothing added or removed. It is usually toasted or processed to remove the unpalatable beany flavor and odor. This soybean flour has a high caloric content because it contains all the natural fat of the soybean, which is approximately 20 percent.

Low-fat or *medium-fat soybean flour:* Part of the fat has been removed, and it may contain from 5 to 8 percent fat.

Minimum-fat or *fat-free soybean flour:* Most of the fat has been removed, and it contains about 1 percent fat.

The protein concentrations in high-fat flour range from 40 to 45 percent. They are higher in both low- and medium-fat flours, ranging from 47 to 54 percent.

The food and beverage industries find many uses for soybean flours. Such flours help to emulsify fats in candy and prevent them from drying out. Brewers have used these flours to help stabilize foam in beer. Bakers have found that they are excellent additions to many of their products. Soybean flours are used in the manufacture of pasta products and many ready-prepared soups. Because of the low starch content, the alkaline ash, and the easy digestibility of the fat, soybean flours are used extensively in many dietary foods, infant foods and special soft-diet foods.

You can use soybean flours in many ways at home. Add them to your recipes in small quantities, as you would add eggs or milk. Begin by using these flours sparingly. Then, experiment with increased amounts. In some recipes you will find that you can use a fairly large quantity of soybean flour and obtain good results. You can make muffins and pancakes from soybean flour exclusively, although the product will not be as light or tasty as when you use a mixture of soybean flour and true grain flours. In using soybean flours, remember that they brown easily; bake goods at slightly reduced temperatures.

Sometimes the labels on packages of soybean flours tell the type, or the amount of fat they contain. If the label on the package lacks such information, you can recognize the type of flour by some of its distinguishing features. Both high- and low-fat soybean flours are a deep yellow color; minimum-fat has a light cream color. Both high- and low-fat flours tend to pack, so it is important to sift them before measuring and to pile them lightly into the measuring cup.

The most precise way of telling the type of soybean flour is to weigh it carefully. First, sift the flour and then pile it lightly by the spoonful into a measuring cup without shaking or tapping the cup. Level off the excess flour with the edge of a spatula.

If your scale is accurate, you need weigh only one cup of flour; otherwise, weigh four cups. Then compare the weights with the following figures:

If one cup of flour weighs 2.1 ounces (60 grams), or if four cups weigh 8.4 ounces (240 grams), it is high-fat; if one cup weighs 2.6 ounces (75 grams), or if four cups weigh 10.4 ounces (300 grams), low-fat; if one cup weighs 4.2 ounces (120 grams), or four cups weigh 16.8 ounces (480 grams), minimum-fat.

Although generally you can interchange the three types of soybean flours in recipes, at times the liquid needs to be adjusted. Usually, the more a soy flour weighs, the greater the amount of liquid it will absorb. However, both high- and low-fat flours are similar in their ability to absorb liquids, so you can use one or the other the same way. But when you use a minimum-fat flour, in most cases you will need to *increase* the liquid. Generally, you will not have to change the amount of shortening in a recipe.

Below is an easy cooky recipe, using all-soybean as the "flour." The recipe will be especially welcomed by individuals who cannot tolerate true grains, although the cooky will be enjoyed by all.

100 PERCENT SOYBEAN FLOUR COOKIES

2 cups high-fat soybean flour
2 eggs
1 cup vegetable oil
1 cup unsulfured molasses
1 cup wheat germ

Blend all ingredients together. The batter should be thin enough to drop from a teaspoon. If it is too thick, thin it with a little water or milk. Drop the batter onto a buttered cooky sheet, allowing ample space for it to spread. Bake at 300° F. until the cookies are brown around the edges. This will take about 10 minutes. Check the first batch for timing, since, as already mentioned, baked goods with soybean flours brown quickly. Makes 4 to 5 dozen cookies, depending on the size.

Other Soybean Products You Can Buy

Soybean grits and soybean flakes are similar in composition to soybean flour, but they are not as finely ground. Soybean grits resemble cornmeal in texture; the flakes resemble rolled oats. Grits tend to absorb more liquid than flakes. Both are bland in flavor and will not alter the taste of the food to which they are added. Use them instead of bread crumbs in meat loaves or meat patties. Add them to a granola-type cereal mix. The grits and flakes are soft and can be eaten without being presoaked or cooked. They give baked products a crisp texture, and they are good as food extenders.

APPLE CRISP WITH SOY GRITS

3 cups apples, sliced, with skins intact
½ cup honey
½ cup wheat germ
6 tablespoons soybean grits or flakes
¼ teaspoon cinnamon
3 tablespoons butter, melted

Arrange the apple slices in a buttered casserole. Drizzle them with honey. Blend together the wheat germ, the grits or flakes, cinnamon and butter into a crumbly mixture and sprinkle it over the honeyed apples. Bake in a hot oven (400° F.) for 20 to 25 minutes. Serve hot or cold, topped with yogurt or sour cream. Serves 6.

Crude soybean oil is particularly good in salad dressings. It is a good source for some of the essential fatty acids. Soybeans contain a valuable fat-soluble substance called lecithin, which is also found in egg yolks. Lecithin is used extensively by food processors as an emulsifier, since it breaks up fat particles and oil globules and spreads them evenly throughout food products. Lecithin is used with many baked products, shortenings, candies and ice cream. In health-food stores it is sold as "soy lecithin granules" or "soy phosphatides." Sprinkle the granules over cereal or stir them into liquids such as milk or juices. Liquid lecithin is also sold. It is very viscous and more difficult to handle than the granules. Below are two recipes for using liquid soybean lecithin.

LECITHIN SQUARES

½ cup liquid soybean lecithin
¼ cup honey
½ teaspoon pure flavoring extract (vanilla, almond or peppermint)
¼ cup milk powder (about)

Stir the soybean lecithin, honey and flavoring extracts together until they are thoroughly blended. Add the milk powder and dust some waxed paper with additional milk powder. Flatten the soybean lecithin ball into a layer ¼-inch thick by patting it with your fingers and palms. Chill. Using a sharp knife, cut the mixture into small squares. Chill again. Makes 2 dozen small squares.

COCONUT-LECITHIN BALLS

½ cup liquid soybean lecithin
¼ cup unsulfured molasses
½ teaspoon pure vanilla extract
¼ cup coconut shreds (about), dried and unsweetened

Stir the soybean lecithin, molasses and vanilla extract together until they are thoroughly blended. Add the coconut shreds. Cut off bits with the tip of a teaspoon and roll them into small balls. Roll the balls in additional coconut shreds. Chill. Makes 2 dozen small balls.

There are many fermented soybean products used traditionally in the Orient, and a few of them are now available in the United States. Tamari, a fermented soybean sauce, tastes somewhat like Worcestershire sauce, and is used as a seasoning. Another is miso, a fermented soybean paste. Dissolved in a small amount of cold liquid, it can be added to soup stock or used in the cooking liquid for brown rice and other whole grains. Fermented soybean products tend to be quite concentrated and salty. Use them sparingly. People on low-sodium diets may need to avoid such products.

The Soybean and You

In these times of rising food prices and meat shortages, many of us have been investigating foods other than traditional ones for protein. Plant proteins, including the soybean, are becoming more familiar and popular. Unfortunately some overenthusiastic individuals hail the soybean as a panacea for all our food problems. It is not. Although it is a nourishing, versatile and economic food, at the same time its limitations must be recognized. No single food, day after day, in many disguises, will provide a balanced diet.

Soybeans, as well as other legumes, are quite indigestible for many people. This, too, is a problem which must be recognized. The Orientals, by insisting that fermented soybean products are more digestible, have been trying to tell us something important, based on their long use of the bean. The United States had a revealing experience with fermented versus nonfermented soybeans in World War II. During the Japanese occupation of Indonesia, the manufacture of tempeh, a fermented soybean product, had been suspended and the tempeh cultures were lost. The United States, in an act of compassion, sent soybeans to New Guinea to feed dislocated Europeans and Indonesians. The shippers failed to realize that nonfermented soybeans were considered indigestible and unpalatable to those people, who were accustomed to fermented ones. When the problem was recognized, arrangements were made to have tempeh cultures and tempeh cakes supplied from Surinam. Shortly thereafter, the soybeans supplied by the United States were converted into familiar acceptable fermented products.

After World War II, a report was prepared on the nutritional aspects of tempeh. A firsthand account concerning tempeh as fare for prisoners of war in Indonesia emphasized that unfermented soybeans had been unpopular as a food because they did not soften well during cooking, and were difficult to digest. The feature of indigestibility in soybeans was especially noticed in the POW camps in Southeast Asia. However, when the soybeans were fermented into tempeh, they were readily acceptable and digested. In retrospect, it is now believed that many prisoners of war owe their very survival to the fact that the soybeans were fermented. Accounts told that even prisoners suffering from dysentery and nutritional edema were able to assimilate fermented soybeans.

At present, the main efforts to popularize soybeans in the United States are *not* with fermented ones such as tempeh, but rather as textured vegetable protein. Such products are *inferior* to traditional sources of animal protein (meat, poultry, fish, milk, cheeses and eggs) in their nutrient quality. They lack the same ideal balance of essential amino acids, and they do not have all of the minerals and trace elements. They do not have the same level of nutrient availability. Presently they cannot be supplemented adequately with these missing nutrients, which are not all specifically known. Even if it were possible to supplement them, the added nutrients would not necessarily be as available as those from animal sources.

Textured vegetable protein is being mixed with ground beef, and appropriately labeled, in various supermarkets. "Ground Beef Plus," "Beef Pattie Mix," "Tasty Burger," "Juicy Burger," "Superburger" and other taggings are required for these meat analogs, which now comprise as much as 25 percent by weight of the mix. The USDA estimated that more than 700 million pounds of soybean products were consumed in 1972. This replaced only a trivial amount of meat and represented only 1 percent of all the meat eaten during that year. However, the use of textured vegetable protein is increasing progressively. Agricultural economists predict that by 1980, Americans will be eating from ten to twenty times as much textured vegetable protein as they are now.

In 1971, USDA approved the use of textured vegetable protein in school lunch programs. The present allowable proportion is slightly more than is being used in the supermarket soybean-beef mix. In the school lunch program, textured vegetable protein can be used up to 30 percent, with 70 percent animal protein. This program has come under sharp attack by some professionals and parents, who feel that this program has cheapened the school program not only in a monetary sense but also in a nutritional one. The Food Research and Action Center, a group of professionals in nutrition, medicine and education as well as concerned citizens, look upon the use of textured vegetable protein in the school lunch program as a step in the wrong direction, in "a long and accelerating trend toward a more and more highly processed diet, consisting of 'mock foods' concocted in the laboratory." . . .

"Clearly the trend of using more fabricated foods does not represent a move toward the rational use of vegetable protein in a world heading toward a shortage of animal protein. It is, instead, a triumph for the food technologists and the food companies. . . . If the American people, knowing the real options and the real risks, choose to take the path toward an increasingly synthetic diet, it is, of course, their privilege. To take them along this path without their informed consent is a serious deception. To allow their children to be taken along this path without their parents' knowledge and consent . . . is a nutritional crime."

In conclusion: Become acquainted with the soybean as a nutritious food with certain limitations. Remember that to make the best possible nutritional choices you should select brown rice rather than white polished rice; natural cheese rather than processed cheese; baking potatoes rather than reconstituted, instant mashed, or fried chips. In the same way, if you use soybeans, select the most nutritious forms rather than as highly contrived "mock foods."

Suggested Reading

Altschul, Aaron M., "The Revered Legume." *Nutrition Today,* Vol. 8, No. 2, March–April 1973, pp. 22–29.

Chen, Philip S., *Soybeans for Health, Longevity and Economy.* South Lancaster, Massachusetts: The Chemical Elements, 1957.

Hunter, Beatrice Trum, *Fermented Foods and Beverages: An Old Tradition.* New Canaan, Connecticut: Keats Publishing, 1973, "Soybeans," pp. 31–49.

King, Seth S., "The Soybean Boom." Sunday *New York Times,* Business and Finance, Section 3, October 29, 1972, pp. 1–2.

Lager, Mildred, and Van Gundy Jones, Dorothea, *The Soybean Cookbook.* New York: Devin-Adair, 1963.

Lanouette, William J., "This Beanstalk Yields Plenty of Jack." *National Observer,* April 14, 1973, pp. 1; 17.

Liener, Irvin E., "Toxic Factors in Edible Legumes and Their Elimination. *American Journal of Clinical Nutrition,* Vol. 11, October 1962, pp. 281–98.

Murphy, W. B., "Some Things You Might Not Know About the Foods Served to Children." *Nutrition Today,* Vol. 7, No. 5, September–October 1972, pp. 34–35.

Rosenfield, Daniel, "What's New in Foods?" *Food and Nutrition,* Vol. 2, No. 2, April 1972, pp. 11–13.

Snider, Nancy, *Soybean Recipe Ideas.* New York: Arco Publishing, 1972.

"Soybean Flour," *Agricultural Research,* April 1966, pp. 8–9.

"Statement Submitted to the USDA Protesting the Use of Alternate Foods in School Food Service." New York: Food Research Action Center, 1973.

"Textured Vegetable Protein in School Lunch Program." *Food Processing,* Autumn, 1971, Special Section, Foods of Tomorrow, pp. F 4–7.

Van Duyne, Frances O., *Recipes for Using Soy Flour, Grits, Flakes and Soybean Oil.* Urbana, Illinois: Extension Service in Agriculture and Home Economics. Circular 664, June 1950.

Van Dyne, Frances O., *Recipes for Using Soybeans: Fresh Green Soybeans and Dry Soybeans.* Urbana, Illinois: Extension Service in Agriculture and Home Economics, Circular 662, June 1950.

10 Satisfying That Sweet Tooth

✤

Whether it is dessert or snacking time, almost everyone has a sweet tooth. Desserts, confections and snacks can be made with foods that are *naturally* sweet, yet high in good nutrients such as minerals and vitamins. Fresh fruits in season make good desserts and snacks; so do dried fruits.

DRIED FRUIT DESSERTS

The natural sweetness of dried fruits appeals to all. Dried fruits are raw, with only the water drawn from them. They are nutritious, and they can add variety to meals especially during the winter in northern regions, where the choices of fresh fruits are limited. You can find dried raisins, figs, dates, prunes and apricots readily. Other dried fruits, sometimes available, but less common, include dried bananas, apples, peaches, pears, cherries and persimmons.

Shopping for Dried Fruits

As with so much of the food shopping today, you'll have to consider nutritional "trade-offs" before choosing between dried fruits that have been treated with sulfur dioxide or those that have been sun-dried. Sulfur dioxide preserves many dried fruits against mold, and helps retain their color as well. In large amounts, sulfur dioxide is very poisonous and highly irritating. This chemical compound is used to treat a number of other foods and beverages, and it is also a frequent air pollutant. The total amount of sulfur dioxide and other sulfur compounds to which you may be exposed from various sources is considerable. The Food and Drug Administration (FDA) considers that the amount of sulfur dioxide used with dried fruits, as well as other foodstuffs, to be self-limiting because the foods or beverages would be so distasteful as to be inedible if high amounts were used. The agency has not set any tolerance levels for sulfur dioxide on foodstuffs, and considers it to be GRAS (Generally Recognized As Safe). This policy is arbitrary as well as unscientific. "Self-limiting" is a fatuous criterion for the use of any chemical in food. A point of harmfulness and toxicity may be reached at a level far below that which affronts the tongue or nose. Even though sulfur dioxide is on the GRAS list, the FDA has asked for further studies regarding its safety.

On the other hand, sulfur dioxide does help to preserve some vitamins in dried fruits, which are drastically destroyed when sun-dried. For instance, there is no loss of vitamin A when fruits are dried with sulfur, and some vitamin C is retained. *Sulfur-dried apricots are considered to be an outstanding source of vitamin A.* In sun-dried apricots there is a complete loss of vitamin C and an appreciable loss of vitamin A; the amount lost is proportional to the color loss. However, sulfur dioxide destroys some of the vitamin B₁. Since figs and prunes contain vitamin B₁ but little vitamin A, *sun-dried figs and prunes are nutritionally superior to those which have been treated with sulfur dioxide.*

Preparing Dried Fruits

Unless the dried fruits are extremely dry and hard, many of them are delicious served as they are. Since they are very concentrated foods, use them sparingly, and drink extra water or other liquid. Also, remember that sticky dried fruits, when retained in the mouth, can be a cavity-forming factor for teeth, along with candies, cookies, honey or molasses.

You can create a number of quick and easy desserts using dried fruits. They combine especially well with all types of nuts and seeds, such as pumpkin and sunflower. Try dried fruits with natural hard cheeses, cottage cheese or ricotta. Fill the centers of prunes, date or figs with nuts, peanut butter, seeds or cheese. To make dried fruits festive, roll them in unsweetened coconut shreds or sesame seeds. Make your own favorite combinations and arrange them on platters, along with succulent fresh fruits. Since dried fruits are sticky to handle, spear them with toothpicks.

If you plan to use dried fruits in compotes, whips or other desserts which require that the fruits be soft, merely soak the dried fruits overnight or for a few hours in warm water. Cooking dried fruits to soften them is unnecessary. Plan to use the water, which will be mineral-rich.

Dried fruits combine well with yogurt or sour cream to make jiffy fruit whips. There are no exact proportions. Make it as thin or as thick as you like. Use any type of dried fruit to substitute for apricots in the following recipe. Or use a combination of dried fruits, or of dried and fresh fruits.

A. P R I C O T   W H I P

Cut up 2 cups of dried apricots and soak the pieces in enough warm water to cover them. After they have softened, turn the fruit and the liquid into an electric blender. Add a few tablespoons of yogurt or sour cream and blend the mixture into a smooth purée. Turn it into 6 sherbet glasses, and garnish with sesame seeds or nuts, either whole or ground. Chill. Serves 6.

F R O Z E N   D A T E   D E S S E R T

This dessert, which tastes very much like ice cream, needs no additional sweetening agent since the dates are naturally sweet.

Remove the pits from 2 cups of dates and cut up. Soak the pieces in 1 cup of warm water until they have softened. Pour 2 cups of light cream into an electric blender and add both the dates and the liquid in which they have been soaked. Add a dash of cinnamon or nutmeg. Blend until smooth. Turn the mixture into 6 freezer-proof custard cups and place them in the freezer. Freeze until firm. Serves 6.

D R I E D   F R U I T   "P I E   C R U S T"

Measure equal parts of pitted dates and fresh coconut and put them through the fine blade of a food grinder. Pat the mixture into a buttered pie plate and shape it into a crust. Chill until it is firm, and then fill with fresh fruits or berries in season. Top with yogurt or sour cream.

DRIED FRUIT COMPOTE

Cover a mixture of any dried fruits in warm water. Add a dash of whatever flavoring you like: cinnamon, nutmeg, clove, allspice or ginger. Mix and allow the fruit to soften and the flavoring to permeate the compote. Serve either at room temperature or chilled, topped with yogurt or sour cream.

Enjoy nature's sweets to top off your meal. It will end in satisfaction—naturally!

CONFECTIONS

Confections, too, can be made with foods that are naturally sweet, including dried fruits. Combined with nuts or seeds, you can make an easy and delicious natural confection.

FRUIT-NUT BALLS

Grind together any dried fruits and nuts in a meat grinder. If the mixture sticks in the grinder, put some nuts through. Mix and shape into small balls, the size of walnuts. The stickiness of the dried fruits will bind the mixture together. Roll the balls in additional ground nuts, or in sesame seeds. Eat these confections as they are, or wrap them in waxed paper and freeze them. Instead of shaping all of the mixture into balls, you can pack some of the mixture into small containers, decorate the top by pressing blanched almonds or dried fruits into them to form a design, and chill. Sliced very thin, this is like an unbaked fruitcake. Such small cakes make welcome gift items. You can also freeze this mixture.

Carob

In addition to fruits, there are other foods that are naturally sweet, appealing and nutritious when used as confections. One is carob. The powder is processed from the sweet pulp found in the long, flat pod of the carob tree, which grows mainly in countries bordering the Mediterranean Sea. The fleshy, sweet-tasting brown pods are allowed to dry to a hard, leathery texture. Then they are handpicked and the pods are "kibbled." This process splits the pod and separates the seeds from the small pieces of broken pod. The hard brown seeds are set aside for processing into gums and commercial products, while the pods are used as a chocolate substitute.

Since the carob pod contains about 50 percent natural sugar, the finely ground powder satisfies that sweet tooth. The sugars found in carob are similar to those found in honey, fruits and vegetables.

Carob has a long history. It was known to early civilizations. It is sometimes called St. John's Bread because it was thought to have been the food that sustained John the Baptist during his wilderness ordeal. In later centuries it was eaten by the poor, especially during periods when bread flours were scarce. Carob pods have always been used extensively to feed cattle. During the

War of 1812, they often were the principal food of the British cavalry horses quartered temporarily in southern Spain. In World War II, the people of southern Greece sustained themselves mainly on carob pods during the German occupation.

In recent times, the nutritional values of carob as a human food have become better appreciated. Carob is an easily assimilated properly balanced alkaline food. It contains significant amounts of vitamins and minerals; has only 2 percent fat, contrasted with 52 percent in chocolate; can be processed without any of the chemical food additives such as artificial colors, flavors, preservatives, hydrogenated fats or sugars; and it does not undergo any harsh chemical processing with alkali.

The flavor of carob is surprisingly similar to chocolate and makes it an ideal substitute for those who wish to, or need to, avoid chocolate. Ongoing clinical investigations at a pediatric allergy clinic indicate that children who are allergic to chocolate are not allergic to carob.

Carob is sold in several forms. The dried pods are also known as "honey locust," "locust bean" and "boecksur." They are moist and pliable when they are fresh. Dried out, they become hard and brittle.

Carob powder is ground from the carob pod, and is sold either plain or roasted. The latter is more palatable. There is great variation both in the price and flavor of carob powders. Some are far less chocolaty than others; a few are flat-tasting and disagreeably gritty. If you are disappointed the first time you try carob powder, don't despair. Switch to another brand, and keep trying until you find one that pleases you.

Carob powder is also sold as "carob flour" but flour is a misnomer. It is not a flour as is a flour from grain; it is merely ground finely.

Carob syrup is a natural sweetener, condensed from carob. Some products are colorless and lack any distinctive chocolaty flavor. They look and taste like corn syrup. Other carob syrup is dark, and does have a chocolaty flavor.

You can combine carob powder with two other natural sweeteners to make the following confection, without adding any traditional sweeteners.

UNCOOKED CAROB MOCK FUDGE

Combine equal amounts of milk powder, dried, unsweetened coconut shreds and toasted carob powder. Blend them together, just moistening with enough water or milk so that the mixture forms a thick paste. There are no rigid proportions for this recipe: If you add too much liquid, just add more dry ingredients; if the paste is too thick, add a little more liquid. If you wish, substitute a little pure vanilla extract for some of the liquid. If you use freshly grated coconut instead of dried coconut, use the clear liquid that comes out of the coconut. After you form the thick paste, pat it down evenly into a square 8-by-8-inch baking pan. Use a rubber spatula to get the sticky mixture off of your palms and fingers, as well as to smooth the top of the mixture. Refrigerate until the mixture is firm. This may take 1 or 2 days, depending on how much liquid you have blended into it. Using a sharp blade, score the mock fudge into 1-inch squares. If you wish, press half a walnut into the center of each. Cut the squares and remove them carefully. They are now ready to eat, or to store in the refrigerator for a limited time. Or wrap individually in squares of wax paper and freeze them. You can also form this mixture into small balls, the size of walnuts, and roll them in additional coconut or sesame seeds. They, too, can be wrapped individually in squares of wax paper and frozen.

Whether you shape these confections of Fruit-Nut Balls and Uncooked Carob Mock Fudge into squares, balls or cakes, plan to make a supply ahead of time. They will be ready for those special occasions of birthdays, parties and holidays. Make a good supply. They go fast!

SNACKS

Singly, nuts, seeds and dried fruits are excellent snacks; combined, they are even better. Try combining any raw, unsalted nuts such as almonds, walnuts, cashews, pecans, pignolias, filberts and others. Add seeds, such as sunflower or pumpkin. Although the peanut is a legume, we think of it as a nut. Add peanuts to any nut-seed mixture. Add any dried fruits. Vary the mixes, and keep them handy in a snacking bowl. Or pack a blend of them in small containers or bags, and either refrigerate or freeze them. By doing this, you will keep the nuts and seeds fresh longer. They can be eaten right from the freezer, and they will be crisp and crunchy.

A little of this snack mixture goes a long way. Take small bags of it with you for brown-bagged lunches, travel, picnics, backpacking, motorcycling—however you travel and wherever you go.

DRYING FRUITS

Although dried apples and pears are sometimes sold, their supply is apt to be irregular, and they are quite expensive. Try drying these fruits at home, especially if you have any surplus fruits in the fall. If any begin to spoil, salvage them by drying.

Wash the fruit but do not peel it. Cut away any spots or bruises. Slice the apples about ⅛ inch thick, cutting from the edge to the core, in three different sets of slicings, so the remaining core is triangular. Add the core to homemade vinegar (see pages 57–58).

Place the apple slices on a cake-cooling rack, without overlapping the fruit. Allow them to air-dry overnight at room temperature. If you have a gentle heat source, such as on the top of a banked fire from a woodstove, or over a pilot light on a gas cookstove, you can dry the apples quickly. Lacking such sources, place them in a cookstove oven with the door slightly ajar. Set the oven heat at the lowest possible degree and leave the apple slices in the oven for 2 to 3 hours. The slices will be satisfactorily dried when they are leathery and pliable, but not moist to the touch. Store them in tightly closed containers and keep them cool and dry. If prepared properly, such dried apple slices will have a long storage life.

Dry pears in a similar way, but slice them, unpeeled, into rounds. The cores are negligible and the seeds can be picked out and discarded.

Dried apples and pears are delicious when eaten as they are. They make a good potato-chip substitute. Add these dried fruits to the snack mix; to cereals; or reconstitute them in warm water and then use them in whips, sherbets, compotes or pies.

Sun-Drying Fruits

If you live in an area where the sun shines regularly, where the humidity is low and where there is relatively little air pollution, try sun-drying some fruits. Sun-drying requires several days. Fruits that sun-dry easily are apples, apricots, cherries, dates, figs, guavas, nectarines, peaches, pears, plums and prunes.

Wash the fruit carefully and leave the skins on, if possible. You will need to slice large fruits, such as peaches or nectarines.

You can dry fully ripe grapes on their stems, and leave cherries unpitted. If the weather is very dry, you can leave fresh apricots whole, with their pits intact. But in most areas, apricots dry more satisfactorily if you cut them in half, remove the pits, and place them on shallow trays or screens, cut sides up. (Remember that sun-dried apricots lose significant amounts of vitamins A and C.)

If the drying fruit is exposed to temperatures that rise above 115° F., transfer them to the shade. It is also necessary to transfer drying fruit indoors before nightfall to prevent condensation from undoing the sun's work during the day.

The fruit will be sufficiently dry when no moisture can be squeezed from a piece of it when cut; when it is rather tough and pliable; and when a few pieces squeezed together separate from each other when the pressure is released. Figs and cherries should be slightly sticky, while other dried fruits are described variously as "suedelike" or "springy." Apricots will be sufficiently dry when the fruit feels dry on the outside but slightly moist inside. If you have freezer space, stop the drying process slightly before this point, by storing half-dried apricots in containers and putting them in the freezer. They will keep their fine color and flavor. Store other dried fruits in airtight containers in a cool dry place.

MAKING DRIED FRUIT "LEATHER"

If you have shopped in cities where Turkish food is sold, or if you have traveled in the Near East, you may have enjoyed "apricot leather," a thin sheet, rolled up, made of dried apricot paste. You can make your own fruit leather, not only of apricots, but of other fruits too.

Mash 1 quart of fully ripened fruits or berries, drain off extra juice and, if necessary, sweeten with honey. Cover trays or a table with heavy clean plastic, securely fastened with tape. Pour a small portion of the puréed fruits or berries onto the plastic so that it is only about ¼ inch thick. Protect it from insects by stretching a piece of clean plastic netting or cheesecloth over the top. Set the table legs in cans of water to prevent crawling insects from ascending. Set the trays or table outdoors in full sunshine and bring indoors in humid weather and at night. Return to the sun for 2 or 3 days, or until, by gentle lifting, you are able to remove the fruit leather in one piece. Dust it lightly with arrowroot flour and roll it up. Refrigerate or place the fruit leather in a container and freeze it. Fruit leather stores well. To use it, snip off small pieces with a pair of sharp kitchen scissors. These pieces are good to eat out of hand, or mixed with fruit salad or snacks.

Remember to combine dried fruits and nuts. They go so well together. Blend them for desserts. Grind them for confections. Mix them for snacks. Dried fruits and nuts are good companions —naturally!

Suggested Reading

Emery, Carla, *Old-fashioned Recipe Book*. Kendrick, Idaho: Carla Emery, 1974.

Hertzberg, Ruth, Vaughan, Beatrice, and Greene, Janet, *Putting Foods By*. Brattleboro, Vermont: Stephen Greene Press, 1973.

Larson, Gena, "Dried Fruits." *Let's Live.* July 1973, pp. 30–35.

MacManiman, G. *Dry it, You'll Like it!* Fall City, Washington: Living Food Dehydrators, Box 546, 1973.

Stoner, Carol, editor, *Stocking Up: How to Preserve the Foods You Grow, Naturally*. Emmaus, Pennsylvania: Rodale Press, 1973.

USDA publications:
Sun Dry Your Fruits and Vegetables. Federal Extension Service, 1958
Vegetable and Fruit Dehydration. Miscellaneous Publications, No. 540, 1944.
Vandercook, Eugene, "Carob—the Nutritious Food that Looks and Tastes Like Chocolate." *Specialty Food Merchandising.* August 1972, p. 42.

11 Of Special Concern

✿

BABY FOODS

You can prepare many baby foods at home easily and inexpensively. You can omit salt, sugar, modified starch, sodium nitrate and nitrite, and other additives presently being used in commercially prepared baby foods.

Mash soft foods such as banana or avocado with a fork, an old-fashioned wooden mallet or a potato ricer. The banana should be completely ripe, with no green on the skin. Brown speckles should have begun to appear on the skin. Use a soft mashed food as a base for adding small quantities of other foods, such as brewer's yeast, yogurt or milk.

When you cook vegetables such as carrots or squash for the family, remove a small portion before you add any salt, sweetening or condiments. Purée the baby's portion in a food mill (see Appendix).

Excesses of nitrates are now found in many plants, due to the excessive use of nitrogen fertilizers. Young infants are particularly susceptible to nitrite poisoning. Spinach contains relatively large amounts of nitrate, a part of which changes to the more toxic nitrite by bacterial action, especially as it ages. Beets, too, contain sizable amounts of nitrate. Presently, some infants' diets exceed nitrate limits considered safe. Do not feed spinach to children under four months of age, and never feed leftover spinach, even if refrigerated, or uncooked spinach which is not really fresh.

Blend pieces of raw fruit, such as apple, pear or peach, in a small quantity of water or milk in an electric blender to make raw applesauce or a purée of fruit. Use it promptly.

Meat protein is readily digested by babies. Cook meat just long enough to sterilize the outside surface and then scrape it with a spoon. Simmer liver briefly, chop it and grind it in an electric blender, together with the liquid in which it was cooked.

Yogurt and cottage cheese are readily accepted by babies.

When a baby is ready for cereal to be added to the diet, you can use a whole grain if you grind it exceedingly fine. Grind millet, for example, in an electric seed mill (see Appendix). Blend the millet flour with a small amount of cold water or milk into a smooth paste, add it to additional liquid, and cook the mixture in an egg poacher or in a custard cup set into a pan of hot water.

If time is short, you can blend enough baby food for several meals and quick-freeze individual portions. But ideally, it is best to prepare the baby's food freshly for each serving.

Suggested Reading

"Baby Food." *Consumer Bulletin,* March 1972; June 1972.

Hunter, Beatrice Trum, *Consumer Beware! Your Food and What's Been Done to It.* New York: Simon and Schuster, 1971, "Baby Foods: What's In Them?" pp. 311–320.

Johnson, Roberta, and Blankinship, Sue, *Mother's in the Kitchen*. Franklin Park, Illinois: La Leche League International, 1971.

Larson, Gena, *Better Food for Better Babies, and Their Families*. New Canaan, Connecticut: Keats Publishing, 1972.

Turner, Mary Dustan, and Turner, James S., *Making Your Own Baby Food*. New York: Bantam Books, 1973.

FREE PAMPHLETS:

Osterizer Guide for Feeding Baby Better, Home Economics Department, John Oster Manufacturing Company, 5055 North Lydell Avenue, Milwaukee, Wisconsin 53217

New York City's Baby Book, A Handbook for Parents. Health Services Administration, Office of Health Education, Department of Health, Room 926, 125 Worth Street, New York, New York 10013

The Modern Baby. Blue Cross Association. 840 North Lake Shore Drive, Chicago, Illinois 60611

BROWN-BAGGING

If you can't face another sandwich at lunchtime, welcome to the club. Sandwiches were invented back in the eighteenth century. Reputedly, John Montague, the Fourth Earl of Sandwich, spent twenty-four hours or more at the gaming table without food other than layers of beef between slices of bread. And people have been eating sandwiches ever since.

There are many ways you can create nourishing and easily prepared lunches without having to place food between two slices of bread.

For example, pack some slices of cold meat or poultry from

Sunday's roast for Monday's brown-bagged lunch. Add some cherry tomatoes and green pepper rings, which are easy to handle. Add an apple and some crunchy fresh coconut, with an individual serving of tomato juice.

For Tuesday, pack a can of sardines and take along a wedge of lemon for the fish. Some stalks of celery and sprigs of parsley make good accompaniments. Add a bunch of grapes, a few walnuts, and an individual serving of milk.

Wedges of hard cheese are easy to manage. Pack them for Wednesday, along with some radishes and cucumber slices. Add an orange or a tangerine, a small package of raisins and an individual serving of unsweetened apple juice.

If you like hard-cooked eggs, vary them by deviling or mixing them with curry, for Thursday's lunch. Watercress goes well with eggs prepared these ways. Add a banana, sunflower seeds and an individual container of yogurt.

If you use a small wide-mouthed thermos, pack it with foods to be kept hot or cold. Cottage cheese travels well in such a thermos. Top bland cottage cheese with some paprika or minced chives when you pack it for Friday's lunch. Add some thinly sliced raw turnips or use them as crackers for spreading the cottage cheese. Take along a pear, some pumpkin seeds and an individual serving of unsweetened orange juice.

If you want some bread with your lunches, take along a bread and butter sandwich. For variety, substitute whole-grain crackers from time to time.

Invent your own combinations. Variety is the spice of brown-bag lunches; it creates an appetite and makes eating both pleasurable and nutritious.

Pack your own food, not only for the working week, but whenever you travel or picnic. It is less expensive than eating out, and will liberate you from limited choices of pizza parlors, frozen-custard stands and curb-service emporia.

Suggested Reading

Beard, James A. & Brown, Helen Evans, *The Complete Book of Outdoor Cookery.* New York: Pyramid Publications, 1967, "Picnics and Cookouts," pp. 225–237.

The Cooking Camper. Campbell Soup Company, Camden, New Jersey 08101

Hunter, Beatrice Trum, *The Natural Foods Primer: Help for the Bewildered Beginner.* New York: Simon and Schuster, 1972, pp. 23–29.

PARTY FARE

Is company coming? Have a few dependable recipes popular with your guests and easy to prepare in advance. Here are two festive-to-serve but quick-and-easy-to-make dishes.

CRUSTLESS CHEESE AND ONION PIE

This is adapted from a Swiss recipe, traditionally served on New Year's Eve with cold sweet cider.

1 scant cup whole or skim milk
3 raw eggs
1 cup any hard natural cheese, cubed
1 tablespoon arrowroot flour
1 tablespoon vegetable oil
  a pinch of your favorite herbs
2 medium onions, chopped coarsely
1 tablespoon sesame seeds

Place the first 6 ingredients in an electric blender and blend until smooth. Turn the mixture into a buttered pie plate. Turn the onions into the mixture and sprinkle the sesame seeds on top. Bake uncovered in an oven preset at 300° F. for 50 to 60 minutes, or until it is firm and golden brown. Cut the pie into wedges; serve it either hot or cold. One pie will serve 2 or 3 people generously. To make several at one time, repeat the same operations in the blender for each pie, and bake them all together. Remember that eggs like to be cooked gently. Although Swiss cheese is used in the traditional recipe, Cheddar, Tilsit or other sharp natural cheeses give more tanginess to the pie.

CHEESE AND TOMATO PIZZA

This is another easy dish to prepare ahead of time. Although it is enjoyed by people of all ages, it is a special favorite of teenagers. They can learn to prepare it.

    your favorite yeast bread dough
  1 cup stewed tomatoes, well drained
  1 cup any hard natural cheese, cubed
  1 tablespoon of your favorite herbs

Butter a shallow cake pan or pie plate, unless you own special pizza-pie pans. Cake and pie plates with a metal strip attached to the center to move around and loosen crust works especially well for removing pizzas. Line the plate or pan with yeast bread dough. You can use a whole-wheat dough, or one made from the Cornell Mix (see pages 104–05). Pat the dough as thinly as you can, and work the dough up the sides of the plate or pan. Allow the dough to rise for at least ½ hour. Then arrange the tomatoes on top of the dough and strew the cheese on top of the tomatoes. Add any herbs you like. Basil or oregano are especially good. Bake the pie in an oven preheated to 400° F. for about 20 minutes, or until the crust and cheese are both golden brown. Cut the pizza into wedges and serve it hot or cold. One pizza will serve 2 or 3 persons generously.

To make several at one time, repeat the operations for each pizza, and bake all of them together. For variety, add pieces of mushrooms, green peppers, celery, meat or other bits of food along with the cheese.

Either the cheese and onion pie or the pizza, along with a mixed salad and some fresh fruit, make an effortless but festive meal. If the dinner hour is moved up unexpectedly, simply keep the pies or pizzas hot in the oven, set at the lowest heat. Both will hold well at 150° F.

Prepare these dishes in advance, and you will have time to be out of the kitchen, enjoying your guests' company.

Teen-age Party Refreshments

The Indiana State Dental Health Association, jointly with the Indiana State Board of Health, suggested that the basic foods which are included in everyday meals should be the basis of well-balanced party refreshments for youngsters. These are some of the "tasty growth-promoting foods" suggested:

—meat and cheese cubes on toothpicks
—meat rolled in a lettuce or cabbage leaf
—celery stuffed with cheese or peanut butter
—hard-cooked or deviled eggs

—meat, fish, cheese or egg sandwiches
—cheese or meat dips with vegetable sticks
—cheese on slices of raw zucchini, turnip or cucumber

"Fruits and vegetables are children's favorites because of pleasing flavors and textures [they state], and they may be served in many combinations of colors and design. They are fun to eat and nature's way to keep the teeth and mouth clean and fresh."

—Sticks: carrot, celery, fresh pineapple, rutabaga, turnip
—Rings: apple, cucumber, green pepper, pimento
—Wedges: cabbage, lettuce, orange, pear, tangerine, tomato
—Flowerettes: cauliflower
—Roses: radishes
—Curls: carrot, celery
—Halves: fresh apricot, peach, plum
—Fruit bowl: apple, banana, grape, orange, pear

"The American Medical Association, American Dental Association and the National Congress of Parents and Teachers have issued official statements discouraging the . . . use of concentrated, sticky sweets and carbonated beverages. . . ."

Drinks made with cold milk add nutrition and flavor to childrens' party fare and are good thirst quenchers at any time. For color scheme or seasonal theme, choose a favorite unsweetened, natural vitamin-rich fruit or vegetable juice:

—Fresh or frozen unsweetened fruit juices
—Whole sweet milk, buttermilk or fortified skim milk
—Punch made by combining unsweetened fruit juices
—Unsweetened fruit-flavored milk drinks

APRICOT MILK DRINK

2 cups apricot nectar, unsweetened
2 cups milk
   dash of nutmeg

Blend together in an electric blender. Chill. Serves 6.

PINEAPPLE JUICE NOG

3 cups pineapple juice, unsweetened
1 cup yogurt, sour cream or buttermilk

Blend together in an electric blender. Chill. Serves 6.

BANANA MILK DRINK

4 ripe bananas
4 cups milk
   dash of cinnamon

Blend together in an electric blender. Chill. Serves 6.

"Crunchy popcorn and protein-rich nuts are natural foods that offer enjoyment as well as needed exercise for teeth and gums. These . . . foods provide good growth and body-building materials, and they are suggested to take the place of too many soft drinks and candies which have little food value and are harmful to good dental health. Children will enjoy these favorite food snacks at school get-togethers, after school, or when the gang drops in."

Suggested Reading

Better Homes and Gardens Casserole Cook Book. New York: Bantam Books, 1969.

Coggins, Carolyn, *The Cookbook of Fabulous Foods for People You Love.* New York: Pyramid Publications, 1967.

Grossman, Elizabeth H., *Specialties of the House.* New York: Simon and Schuster, 1960.

Hillman, Libby, *New Lessons in Gourmet Cooking.* New York: Hearthside Press, 1971.

Hunter, Beatrice Trum, *The Natural Foods Primer: Help for the Bewildered Beginner.* New York: Simon and Schuster, 1972, pp. 20–23.

Kreipke, Karen, *Nutritious Summer Snacks.* College Station, Texas: Texas A & M University, release, August 16, 1972.

Marsh, Dorothy, and Brock, Carol, *Good Housekeeping Party Book.* New York: Harper & Row, 1958.

O'Connor, Hyla, *Quick and Easy Gourmet Recipes.* New York: Arco Publishing, 1970.

Smackin' Good Snacks: A Nutrition Guide. Indianapolis, Indiana: Indiana State Board of Health (undated).

Springer, Sally, *Snack Foods Can Be Nutritious.* College Station, Texas: Texas A & M University, release, July 12, 1972.

MAKING GOOD FOODS
EVEN BETTER

You can make good foods even better by boosting them nutritionally. Try one suggestion at a time and use moderation.

Learn to combine complete proteins with incomplete ones. Lentils and beans, for example, are good foods but they have incomplete protein. If you add some hard-cooked eggs to a lentil salad, or bits of meat or fish, you have boosted the lentils' protein value by adding complete protein. Or, if you make black bean soup, add some grated cheese to boost its protein value.

Almost everyone likes ground beef patties. You can "beef it up" by learning to use a nutritious organ meat along with the beef. Ask your butcher to grind a beef heart with 1½ pounds of lean ground beef. The heart will not noticeably change the appearance or the taste of the ground beef.

You can beef up ground beef in other ways. Instead of binding the mixture with bread crumbs, add some wheat germ, soybean grits or flakes and raw egg. All of these ingredients will boost the protein value as well as bind the mixture.

Vary the flavor of basic ground beef by using different seasonings and herbs, minced parsley, chopped mushrooms, onions, green peppers, cut carrots, celery, or whatever else you like. Vary the shape by forming the mixture into meat loaf, meatballs, the popular patties, or stuffing the mixture into green peppers or tomatoes.

Peanut butter is another popular food which can be a good vehicle for nutritional boosters. Add soy lecithin granules (see page 167) for a crunchy taste. Protein powders, brewer's yeast or wheat germ will go largely undetected in peanut butter. Even bone meal or kelp powder can be blended into peanut butter if you use small amounts. Add only one such item at a time.

The batter for breakfast pancakes can be a vehicle for "camouflage cooking." Boost the batter's protein value by adding milk powder as well as fluid milk, use extra eggs, yogurt, wheat germ or cottage cheese.

Wheat germ can be added to foods in many ways. Try it in some of the following:

—sprinkled over soft-boiled eggs or beaten into eggs for omelets
  or French toast
—sprinkled over hot or cold cereals
—substituted for bread crumbs in meat patties, meatloaves, poultry stuffing, casserole toppings, apple crisp
—added to bread dough or batter for cakes, muffins, waffles or
  cookies

Adjust your favorite recipes by substituting more nutritious ingredients for those traditionally used:

—for each cup of bleached white flour, use 1 cup of Cornell Mix
  (see pages 104–05); ⅞ cup of whole-wheat pastry flour; or ¾ to
  1 cup of finely ground general purpose whole-wheat flour
—for each tablespoon of white flour as a thickener, use ½ teaspoon of arrowroot starch
—for each tablespoon of sweetened, artificially flavored and colored ready-mix gelatin dessert, use 1 tablespoon of plain gelatin
  and a pint of unsweetened fruit juice, plus pieces of fresh
  fruits
—for each cup of uncooked polished white rice, use 1 cup of uncooked brown rice, unpearled barley, buckwheat groats, bulgur
  or millet
—for each cup of white sugar, use ¾ cup of honey and reduce the
  liquid by ¼ cup; or one cup of sorghum syrup; or 1¼ to 1½
  cups of maple, carob or malt syrups
—for each cup of firmly packed brown sugar, use 1 cup of firmly
  packed date sugar
—for each cup of solid shortening, use ⅔ cup of unrefined vegetable oil
—for each teaspoonful of salt, use a teaspoonful of sea salt, earth
  salt, vegetable salt or ground kelp; better yet, reduce the amount
  of any salt to a bare minimum
—for each square of bitter chocolate, use 3 tablespoons of carob

powder plus a tablespoon each of milk (or water) and vegetable oil

—for each teaspoon of vanillin, use 1 teaspoon of pure vanilla extract

Brewer's Yeast

Brewer's yeast earned its name because originally it was a brewing industry by-product. Currently, brewer's yeast, grown especially for human consumption, is sometimes called "nutritional yeast" or "primary yeast."

Brewer's yeast, a tiny cell from the yeast plant, is one of the universe's smallest units of living matter. The yeast cell is identical in composition to many cells in the human body. It is an outstanding source of nutritional value.

Dr. Clive M. McCay, of Cornell University, in *Yeasts in Feeding,* reported that he was able to double the life span of rats by feeding them brewer's yeast. Dr. McCay noted: "Extensive use of yeast has been made in studies in the field of gerontology, the study of old age. Rats have been employed throughout these attempts to determine the interrelationships between diet and aging. In the first studies in which the extreme span of life of the animals was extended, all animals were fed a diet throughout life containing 5 percent of dried yeast. The oldest animal in this study exceeded 1,400 days of age, whereas the average animal lives about 700 days."

People tend to confuse brewer's yeast with bakers' yeast. Brewer's yeast does not have the leavening power of bakers' yeast. Bakers' yeast, in its unbaked state, is undesirable as human food. It is a live yeast, able to retain thiamine (vitamin B_1). In fact, baker's yeast may even capture some thiamine from other foods and sweep it out of the human body. Because of this characteristic, if you eat live baker's yeast, your body's thiamine supply becomes *depleted.* Brewer's yeast, which has no live cells, does *not* interfere with thiamine absorption. On the contrary, brewer's yeast surrenders its supply of thiamine when digested in the human stomach and upper intestine, and is thus a *source* of thiamine.

Brewer's yeast is sold in many health-food stores and in specialty sections of supermarkets. The powder form is more potent than the flake, but more difficult to dissolve in cold liquids. To compensate, use a little more of the flake than of the powder. The flavor differs from brand to brand; some are more palatable than others. If you sample one and don't like it, try another. Always store brewer's yeast in tightly closed containers, away from light, in a cool, dry place. Brewer's yeast will keep for a long time unrefrigerated.

Brewer's yeast is one of the best nutritional aids, but you have to learn how to use it. At first, try a small amount. Be prepared to experiment. Everyone finds favorite ways to use it. Some like brewer's yeast in tomato juice or soup; it adds both flavor and nutrition. Food processors have been using brewer's yeast for such purposes. It should become better known and used at home, as well.

Some people like to use brewer's yeast mixed with water, milk, or in a milk drink. The following is a palatable pick-me-up. Both the brewer's yeast and milk powder boost the protein of the liquid milk. The banana makes the drink thick and creamy. The molasses, which overpowers the yeast flavor, also provides nutrients.

MILK SMOOTHIE

1 cup milk
1 teaspoon brewer's yeast
2 tablespoons milk powder
½ banana
1 tablespoon unsulfured molasses

Blend all the ingredients together in an electric blender until smooth. Chill. Serves 1.

Fruit juices combine well with brewer's yeast to make refreshing drinks. Unsweetened apple or grape juice can be substituted for the pineapple juice in the following recipe.

PINEAPPLE JUICE FLIP

½ cup pineapple juice, unsweetened
½ cup yogurt
 1 teaspoon brewer's yeast

Blend all the ingredients together in an electric blender until smooth. Chill. Serves 1.

In these days of growing concern about sources of good-quality protein, brewer's yeast may become a food "crop" of worldwide importance. Vast amounts of food yeast can be grown in factories that occupy very little of the earth's surface, for this is a soilless crop. We have learned how to fix nitrogen from the air into simple organic compounds such as ammonia or urea. Yeast can finish the conversion of these compounds into edible protein. We have also learned how to make soluble carbohydrates from plants. Yeast gives us the possibility of making high-quality foods and feeds from forests, combined with minerals dug out of the earth and nitrogen drawn from the air. Yeasts can even be grown on organic residues from canning wastes. This technique can solve two important current concerns: the prevention of pollution and the means of producing enough good food to feed the world. Our concern about ways to improve our individual nutrition must be extended to the larger concern of finding ways to improve human nutrition on a global scale.

Suggested Reading

Anderson, Beth, " 'Sneaky Nutrition' Honest Way to Child's Health." *The Daily Item,* Port Chester, New York, May 16, 1973, p. 29.

Gerard, Ralph W., editor, *Food for Life.* Chicago: University of Chicago Press, 1952, "The Improvement of Human Nutrition, pp. 265–302.

Goetz, Arlene, " 'Camouflage Cooking' to Add Some Nutrition." *Washington Post,* September 14, 1972, pp. D1–2.

Hammond, Lucy T., *Mixes Made at Home,* Lexington, Kentucky: University of Kentucky, Cooperative Extension Service, June 1971.

Hunter, Beatrice Trum, *The Natural Foods Primer: Help for the Bewildered Beginner.* New York: Simon and Schuster, 1972, "How Do You Adjust Your Favorite Recipes?" pp. 110–20.

USDA publications:

Food and Life, USDA Yearbook, 1939

Food for Families with School Children, Home & Garden Bulletin No. 13, July 1963

Food for Fitness, A Daily Food Guide, Consumer & Food Economics Research Division, Agricultural Research Service, May 1967

Food, USDA Yearbook, 1959

Nutrition, Food at Work for You, Consumer & Food Economics Research Division, Agricultural Research Service, December 1971

Your Money's Worth in Foods, Home & Garden Bulletin No. 183, December 1970

Appendix

✤

Here is a list of suppliers for certain utensils and ingredients specifically mentioned in the text.

VEGETABLE STEAMERS

Vegetable steamers are sold in many health-food stores and specialty shops. For stainless steel steamers, write to:

Dione Lucas Gourmet Centers
Bevis Industries, Inc.
Westmoreland Avenue
White Plains, New York 10606

Vita-Saver Inc.
912 Isabel Street
Burbank, California 91506

SOAPSTONE GRIDDLES

Write to:

Barth's Colonial Gardens
Valley Stream, New York 11580

New Hampton General Store
Box 71
Hampton, New Jersey 08827

Vermont Country Store
Weston, Vermont 05161

Vermont Soapstone Company, Inc.
Perkinsville, Vermont 05151

GRINDING MILLS

Health-food stores sell portable electric mills suitable for grinding small quantities of seeds, nuts and grains. Among those commonly sold are:

Mill-A-Mat:
Phoenix Company
30 Vesey Street
New York, New York 10007

Mitey Mill:
Stur-Dee
238 Livingston Street
Brooklyn, New York 11201

Moulinex:
Varco, Inc.
91 Broadway
Jersey City, New Jersey 07306

Suppliers of electric grain-grinding mills (adjustable for coarse cereal, meal or fine flour) are:

All-Grain Electric Grinding Mill:
R & R Hardware
176 West Main Street
Tremonton, Utah 84337
and

Smithfield Implement Company, Inc.
99 North Main Street
Tremonton, Utah 84337

All-Purpose Electric Grain Mill:
Barth's Colonial Gardens
Valley Stream, New York 11580

Miracle Exclusives, Inc.
16 West 40 Street
New York, New York 10018

Gallé:
Gallé Getreidemuhlen (manufacturer—information booklet written in German)
Klosterbergstrasse 27
7742 St. Georgen
Schwartzwald,
Germany

Full of Life Food Products, Inc. (distributor)
40 Central Park South
New York, New York 10019

Hol-Grain Mill:
Hol-Grain Mill
161 West Wisconsin Avenue
Milwaukee, Wisconsin 10019

Lee Household Flour Mill:
Lee Engineering Company
2023 West Wisconsin Avenue
Milwaukee, Wisconsin 53200

Lynco National:
Lynco
Box 15
Filer, Idaho 83328

Magic Mill (although this mill is electrified, it can be converted to hand operation):
   Magic Mill, Inc.
   311 Main Street
   Filer, Idaho 83328

   R & R Hardware
   176 West Main Street
   Tremonton, Utah 84337

Meadows Household Stone Burr Mill:
   North Wilkesboro, North Carolina 28659

Perma-Pak:
   40 East 2430 South Street
   Salt Lake City, Utah 84115

Vita-Mix Corporation Gristmill (this machine is a combination grinder-juicer)
   Vita-Mix Corporation
   8615 Usher Road
   Cleveland, Ohio 44138

Suppliers of hand-grinding mills (principally intended for coarse meal or cereal) are:

All-Grain Stone Hand Mill (rustproof and reported to have special stones designed for slow turning to provide a fine-textured flour the first time through):

   R & R Hardware
   176 West Main Street
   Tremonton, Utah 84337

Big Bell No. 2:
   Erewhon Trading Company
   342 Newbury Street
   Boston, Massachusetts 02115

Corona Hand Mill (heavy duty, made of cast iron):
  Lander, Frary & Clark (manufacturer)
  New Britain, Connecticut 06050
  R & R Hardware (distributor)
  176 West Main Street
  Tremonton, Utah 84337

  Smithfield Implement Company, Inc. (distributor)
  99 North Main Street
  Smithfield, Utah 84337

Gallé De Luxe Model Household Mill (this machine is a stone grinder, designed to be attached to a flat surface, for finely ground flour as well as cereal; it weighs about 15 pounds):

  Full of Life Food Products, Inc.
  40 Central Park South
  New York, New York 10019

Gallé Mini Grain Mill (this machine is a stone grinder which is portable and designed to grind grains coarsely for cereal; it weighs about 4 pounds):
  (address above)

Hand Grinding Mill (a small steel burr mill that clamps onto a table):
  Walnut Acres
  Penns Creek, Pennsylvania 17862

Kruska Mill:
  Nelson and Sons, Inc.
  Box 1296
  Salt Lake City, Utah 84410

Lynco National:
  Lynco
  Box 15
  Filer, Idaho 83328

Magic Mill:
   Magic Mill, Inc.
   311 Main Street
   Filer, Idaho 83328
Quaker City Grinding Mill:
   Quaker City Grinding Mill
   4054 Ridge Avenue
   Philadelphia, Pennsylvania 19129

YEAST

If you cannot find the yeasts described in the text, write to the following for the names of retailers nearest you:

   El Molino Mills
   City of Industry, California 91746
   (for El Molino Dry Yeast Granules)

   Standard Brands, Inc.
   625 Madison Avenue
   New York, New York 10022
   (For Fleischman's Active Dry Yeast For Bakers)

   Universal Foods Corporation
   433 East Michigan Street
   Milwaukee, Wisconsin 53201
   (For Red Star Baking Yeasts)

SOURDOUGH

   Sourdough Jack's Kitchen
   603 Tennessee Street
   San Francisco, California 94107

   Uncle John
   Box 3276
   Midland, Texas 79704

HOPS

If you cannot pick your own hops, order dried hops by mail from:
   Nichols Garden Nursery
   Pacific North
   Albany, Oregon 97321

FOOD MILLS FOR BABY FOODS

You can find small Foley Mills in many stores. If not, contact Foley Manufacturing Company, 3300 Fifth Street, N.E., Minneapolis, Minnesota 55418 for the name and address of the nearest supplier.

Happy Baby Food Grinder, made by Bowland-Jacobs Manufacturing Company, Spring Valley, Illinois 61362, is intended for the preparation of small portions of cooked vegetables and meats at the table. The hand grinder consists of a white plastic hopper with a 4-ounce capacity and a handle that turns a small perforated metal disk and blade. Instructions given for its use are clear. The device can be disassembled easily, washed in a dishwasher and readily reassembled. The grinder is small enough to be carried on trips, stored in its original box, which measures only 4¾″ by 3¾″ by 3¾″. Many health-food stores sell this food grinder.

Index

✤

(